We Survived Yesterday

or

The Baja Expedition

John Reseck, Jr.

Griffin Publishing
Glendale, California

Editorial/production supervision: Richard D. Burns
Interior design/formatting: Mark M. Dodge
Cover design: The Creative Type
Copy editor: Dina Falls
Typesetting: RB Author Services

ISBN 1-882180-18-6

Co-publishers
Reseck Enterprises
631 Montgomery Lane
Port Ludlow, WA 98365

Manufactured in the United States of America.

Preface

This is a true story about the adventure of four men paddling two double kayaks over one thousand miles, from San Diego, California to Cabo San Lucas, Baja California. It seems only two people had ever completed the entire distance before and no one had done it in a double kayak.

What made this trip an adventure rather than just an expedition taken by sea kayakers is the rugged, exposed coastline. The entire trip was in open ocean and every night when we came ashore we had to contend with the Pacific swell as it hit the bottom and changed to breaking whitewater surf. The swell rolls across the Pacific Ocean from unknown storms on unknown shores as far away as Asia. It can be two feet high and gently caress the shore or it can be a series of monstrous sixteen foot giants in search of a beach to destroy. As we were to find out, a wave of only eight feet has the power to smash our slender boats like toothpicks if we are caught under it as it peaks and crashes forward in a wall of white, churning foam.

Just as the surf tested our skills each night as we paddled with the waves to come ashore, so our competence and strength were tested each morning as we struggled to punch our way through the breakers to reach the safe zone beyond the surf instead of being washed backwards and tossed up on the beach. Even this trial would be of no great concern to skilled paddlers, but the shore line in many areas consists of cliffs and rocks with no place to camp above the rising water during high tide. This translated into anticipating spending some nights at sea continuing to paddle until daylight. To attempt a landing in darkness through the surf on an unknown beach would be insane.

The other parameter which added difficulty to the trip was self-imposed. It was the time restriction of forty days. This meant that we would have to paddle thirty miles a day in order to have six days to spend on the beach to escape storms and bad weather. Again, a thirty mile day is not that difficult as one day, but thirty-five of them one after another could turn out to be a bit of a chore, both physically and mentally.

I am fifty-seven years old. I put this trip together to fulfill a dream. This account of the trip is my personal perception of what happened and why. Escape with me in the fulfillment of my dream. A thousand mile paddle into, "The Baja Adventure," where all we had to do was "survive yesterday."

Contents

A Word of Thanks

This expedition fulfilled a dream. A word of thanks to some of those that helped in its realization.

To those that traveled with me, Jan, Dave and Glenn, I say, "Gracias compadres!"

To those that read the manuscript and made corrections, my son John III, Marge Dieterich, Ron Jesser and Richard Clucas, I say, "Thank you!"

To my wife who put up with a year of preparation and drove to Cabo to pick me up, I say, "I love you."

To all the pescaderos we encountered on our voyage, I say, "Hasta luego simpaticos."

Introduction

I am writing this section of the book before the trip. This is important because I may feel very different about a lot of things after the trip and I don't want these changed feelings to influence what I write here. To be worthwhile, an experience must change you in some way. Only time will tell if this adventure will be worthwhile.

WHY?

The most often asked question when I mention my planned Baja trip is, "Why do you want to do that?" The second question asked is almost always, "How do you go to the bathroom in a kayak?" These are both excellent questions.

When Sir Edmund Hillary was asked the same question of why he climbed mountains, he became famous when he quoted George Leigh Mallory's statement and said, "because it is there." I found myself not as clear in understanding my desire to paddle Baja as Mallory and Hillary had been of their desire to climb mountains. I didn't have a logical answer to why I would take a large financial loss by retiring early, getting up every morning and working out hard for an hour or more for eight months, spending $7,000.00 on equipment and supplies, and leaving my happy home for six weeks just so I could be uncomfortable in a kayak paddling ten hours a day for forty days. If I completed the trip healthy and uninjured, and if my camera didn't break, I would be able to give a slide show to my friends. Big deal!

I became embarrassed at the lack of understanding of my own motivation to the point of spending a great deal of time thinking about it. Now *I* think I understand why I have to do it, but I'm not sure I can put it into words others will understand. It started a long time ago......

"It will be a good trip for you, honey. It'll let you put all this wanderlust behind you. Just be careful and don't take any chances." My mother was talking to her twenty-two year old son. I had just told her I was going to the Antarctic as a marine biologist to participate in the International Geophysical Year. It was 1957. That expedition was this lower middle class boy's first taste of truly "walking the edge."

Conditions were primitive then. We were allowed one shower every ten days. We slept in tents called Jamesways. The Jamesways' were a two layer canvas tent with insulation in between the layers. They were the shape of a metal quonset hut about twelve feet wide and thirty feet long. Each one had thirteen men assigned to it. They had an oil stove in one end and along the sides some steel bunk beds with sagging rusted springs covered by two inch thick stained cotton pads for mattresses. There was no circulation in the tent and the top bunk was 80 degrees Fahrenheit while the bottom one was 40 degrees Fahrenheit. If you had a bottom bunk you slept in your sleeping bag. If you had a top bunk you slept on top of it.

I spent a lot of my time sitting on the ice next to a twelve inch hole dug with a three inch ice chisel welded on to the end of a five foot steel rod trying to catch fish for the scientific collection. Seven people died on the expedition due to accidents. One fell into a crevasse and six died in a plane that crashed on take off from the ice. For me it was my first taste of true adventure.

Instead of putting my wanderlust behind me like my mother thought it would, it opened an entire new world to me. It was a world, unfortunately, that she never understood. This thirst for adventure, for being the first to do something, or like Don Quixote "to reach the impossible dream," never left me. It isn't very often you get the opportunity to be the first to do something, but you can enlarge on your own experience and challenge your own ability anytime you've got the spunk to do it.

Let's say you've been on the same job ten years. Everything is going well and the job is easy because you have worked out all the angles to get the highest production with the least effort. Things are really good, you don't have to work hard, and your pay is good. Guess what? You are in the comfort trap. What's that you say? "I worked hard to get here!" That's true and you are being very productive for someone else, but your personal growth has come to a complete halt. When you are doing something you do well, you are not learning. You only learn when you struggle.

We don't need to learn very much to just survive. With a little more effort we can learn enough to be comfortable. Most people stop right there. For them being comfortable is their goal in life. Other people, and I count myself as one of them, become uneasy and bored when everything is "comfortable."

For a long time I didn't understand this restlessness and was unhappy because I didn't enjoy living the "good life" my friends were enjoying. I went to the same parties, did the same things, had the same amount of money;—why were they so happy while I was restless? I talked to some of them about it. They said I was going through a typical middle age crisis. I was forty.

I tried to get them to join me in my happy place which was the woods, camping in a tent and sleeping on the ground. They would come with me, *once*. It definitely was beyond their comfort zone. They would tell me what a great time they had, they were glad they did it but not again, thanks.

I talked three of my good friends into going to Alaska with me to fish for salmon in the Brooks River. They stayed in the lodge and ate at the restaurant. I camped in my tent and ate off my one burner stove in the rain. One of them asked me why I didn't stay at the lodge with them. I said, "It's too expensive." Another one of them looked me right in the eye and said, "If you had all the money in the world you would still be right where you are now, in the campground sleeping on the ground." I realized he was right—and then rather sadly, that I was truly different from my friends. I also realized that at least one of them was aware of that fact before I was.

Once I became aware that my values were different from most other people that I came in contact with, I was no longer confused. Like most things in life, it was not a question of right or wrong, just a fact that what was important out of life for me was not the same for them. It was a subtle difference on the surface, but it translated into a major difference in lifestyle, a difference that works out well for me.

Most people share the same values and are often found in the same place doing the same thing at the same time. That's why there are fourteen million people in the Los Angeles basin. That leaves a lot of room for me on the ocean in my kayak, or in the mountains with my backpack.

Just to prove to you how really weird I am, I don't own a stereo system, or a cellular phone. I drive a Suzuki Samari (and like it), my wife and I get along just fine, and if I have a choice I would rather eat at home than go out for dinner. Because of all these modern cultural negatives I only have a handful of close friends. They are a very tolerant group.

My awakening that it was okay to be different allowed me to do things that seem stupid to others (including my tolerant friends). A good example would be the sweat lodge I built in my back yard out of sticks I cut myself, and mud I carried into my back yard in buckets from twenty miles away because it had to be the right texture to mix with straw to make a plaster. When it was finished a dinner guest saw it in my back yard and innocently mistook it for a compost pile. I wasn't the least bit offended—it looked like one. I thought it was beautiful. I'm not sure why I felt I had to build it, but I did. Like so many experiences in life I'm not sure what I learned by building it, but I know it was something I could have learned in no other way and that I was a changed and better person for having completed it.

I think most people have felt the drive to do something that was considered ridiculous by their friends and because they feared their friend's negative comments and lack of understanding, they didn't do it. Too bad. There was so much they could have learned that they missed out on.

There's an old joke that goes like this: "When we're twenty years old we worry about what everyone thinks of us. When we're forty years old we tell everyone we don't care what they think of us. When we're sixty years old we realize that no one has been thinking about us anyway."

You may not realize it but now you know why I'm doing this kayak adventure. Let's create a list of some good reasons that would be important to me. (Or perhaps I should say let's try to extract some logic out of this hodgepodge you have just read.)

A FEW GOOD REASONS TO GO

1. I've given myself permission to do it.
2. I want to do it.
3. I don't know if I am physically able to do it.
4. I don't know if I am psychologically able to handle it.
5. People advised me not to do it.
6. There is nothing to gain from it.
7. It will be the most difficult thing I have done up to this point in my life.
8. I can be the first to do it in this type of boat.
9. We can possibly set a time record for others to shoot at.

With my set of values any one of these would be motivation enough to do it, but alas, there is one more that is probably the real reason.

One of the things I hold sacred is that an individual is only as good as his word. (The one thing all my friends have in common is that I would trust any of them with my life.) I was sitting in the patio of an old friend and said, "Someday I am going to paddle around Baja in a kayak." At that time I owned a fabric covered Folbot that I had made from a kit at home in my garage. The year was 1961. The old friend is dead now, but that doesn't change anything. I told him I was going to do it. I gave my word. It has just taken me a lot longer than I had expected to get ready.

WHO?

When you plan a "walk on the edge" for yourself, it is important whom you plan it with. I have a rule that I try to follow. The closer to the edge I plan to walk, the farther from the edge I want the people with me to walk. For example, if I wanted to climb Mount Rainier in Washington State my preferred partner would be Sir Edmund Hillary. For me that climb would be a true "walk on the edge." For Hillary it would be an afternoon stroll.

On this kayak trip I am not on a razor's edge so I don't need Ed Gillet, who paddled from California to Hawaii, or Hannes Lindemann, who paddled across the Atlantic. I do, however, need people I can depend on to be at least as good and preferably better than I am. The three men who will share the Baja adventure with me are all very special.

Two of them are in their mid twenties and, of course, that makes them immortal (like I was when I was in my mid twenties). The third one is fifty-two but still thinks he's in his mid twenties, so he is all right too.

Glenn Pinson, one of the young ones, will be in the front of my boat. Glenn and I met at Rancho Santiago

College in Santa Ana, California, where I was teaching SCUBA diving and he was a student. Glenn was different in that he listened when I talked, (this is rather an unusual trait among students). Glenn was studying fire science and took up SCUBA not just as a hobby, but also as a skill which could be used in firefighting. After he was certified as a diver he became my assistant and my beach lifeguard.

I was immediately impressed with him because he was always where he was supposed to be, on time and ready to work. He took life seriously, but not himself. He left our college to become a firefighter with the Beverly Hills Fire Department. In his spare time he became a mountaineering instructor and a kayak instructor.

Glenn had paddled, with a friend, from the town of San Felipe in the north east corner of Baja California to Cabo San Lucas at the southern tip of the Baja Peninsula. This inside passage is a long, but not an intense paddle. I still have to do that one to fulfill my promise to paddle "around" Baja California. Glenn has to do our outside paddle to complete the same dream.

Glenn's skills in boat handling are better than mine, but I am stronger than Glenn. When we need power, I will supply it. When we need finesse, it's up to him.

In the other boat will be Dave Seymour and Jan Richardson. Dave is similar to Glenn in that he is still immortal. Dave and Jan have paddled together for a long time and have accomplished some extraordinary things in their kayaks. Dave found the water fairly calm one day crossing the channel from Ventura on the California coast to Anacapa Island, a distance of twelve and one-half nautical miles, so he paddled it backwards to break the boredom. Like I said, he's the young one. Dave is a kayak instructor, a tour leader, and a cyclist. I met Dave through Jan at the college. Dave takes classes there. When Jan told me he had a kayaking partner that he did most of his paddling with, I was impressed, because Jan is the strongest paddler I know. I thought, "this Dave guy must be a real hunk like Jan."

When I met Dave he didn't fit my preconceived image. I thought, "he doesn't look exceptionally strong." He was tall and lean. When I paddled with Dave I found that his skill with the paddle made up for any lack of upper body bulk. He left me in his foam. Since then we have become friends and I am still impressed by him. Before I tell you of some trips Dave and Jan have taken together, let me tell you a bit about our fourth paddler, Jan Richardson.

Jan is the other oldie on the trip. He is fifty-two but, as I said earlier, he still thinks he is in his twenties. There is nothing he enjoys more than going into the weight training room at the college and outlifting all the young studs. He has run several ultra-marathons (fifty plus miles), is a kayak guide and a Velodrome cyclist. He can be found almost any afternoon running around in his shorts, lifting weights, and driving the women wild with his sweaty "Charles Atlas" body. When Jan pulls a paddle through the water, the ocean moves backwards. He is the power in the second boat. Dave is the finesse.

Jan and Dave decided to paddle from Newport Beach, California, to Avalon on Catalina Island (twenty-six nautical miles offshore. Jan asked, "John, why don't you come along?" I had not been paddling seriously for very long and that would have been an "edge walk" for me. I thought about saying yes, but knowing the way Jan and Dave paddle I was worried about being able to keep up.

I was also worried at my age and physical condition if I could recover in time to paddle back the next day. I thought perhaps they might spend two days in Avalon and then I knew I'd recover okay. So I asked, "When are you paddling back?"

Jan said, "Well, if we leave Newport Beach by five o'clock in the morning, we should be able to get to Avalon by noon. We'll grab a hamburger and start back at one. That should get us back to Newport Beach around eight or nine o'clock." I declined this wonderful opportunity to torture myself.

They completed the paddle even though they had to fight low visibility and rough water all fifty plus miles. They don't know for sure how far they paddled. They worked against the seas on the way over and ended up a few miles north of Avalon because they couldn't see land. On the way back they came in a few miles south of the harbor and had to paddle back. They got back at eleven o'clock at night, cold and very tired.

The other trip they took, which I also wisely declined, was from Newport Beach to San Diego, California, non-stop. This is an eighty-six mile trip. All of it is open sea, and it took them twenty-two hours. I picked them up in a car in San Diego.

A record that Jan proudly holds is the record time running from the Dead Sea in Israel to the top of Massada in the summer—in 110 degree heat. Like I said, he still thinks he is twenty years old.

When Glenn called me on the phone and said, "John, I hear you are retiring at the end of the school year. Does that mean you're ready for the west coast of Baja?" He had heard me talking about wanting to paddle around Baja for years.

I said, "Yes." I knew Glenn would be a good partner. When I thought more about the trip, I thought, "John, cover your ass. Ask Jan and Dave to go, too." Then if your body falls apart the three of them can tow you home." I didn't know if I could talk Dave and Jan into it, but I thought I'd give it a try.

I said, "Jan, Glenn Pinson and I are going to paddle the west coast of Baja next year." Before I could go on Jan said, "Ed (Ed Gillet, the Hawaii paddler) told me that was one of the hardest paddles he had ever made. (Ed is one of only two people to have ever completed this paddle and they did it together in single kayaks.) Can I go with you?"

I played it cool and said, "Well, I guess so. Do you think Dave might want to go?"

"I'll ask him," and Jan was off. Jan called me that evening and said that we could count Dave in. My comfort zone had just increased. I was surrounded by skilled, dependable people that I knew would take good care this old curmudgeon.

Only three steps remained:
1. Select the equipment, (ouch to the bank account).
2. Get the old body in shape (ouch everywhere).
3. Start paddling.

WITH WHAT?

At the time we decided the trip was a "go," and the four of us were locked in, I owned three different kinds of kayaks. I had a folding fabric covered boat, a plastic boat, and a Kevlar boat (Kevlar is like fiberglass but stronger and lighter). I gave a lot of thought to which boat would be the best.

I ruled out the fabric boat because I had smashed one a few years before under a ten foot wave. The frame broke in half and I knew that every night and every morning on our trip it would be heavy surf time. I didn't think the fabric boat would stand up to that kind of pounding. I jumped to the conclusion that the Kevlar boat would be the best choice. It was light, fast, and held a lot. It was a "Tesla" made by Necky Kayaks in British Columbia, Canada.

The more I studied the charts and talked to people that knew the Baja coast, (I know it well myself), the more I realized that the plastic boat may be the better choice. At least half our beach landing would be on rocks. The plastic boat could take that kind of abuse much better than the fiberglass or regular Kevlar. So I changed my mind and decided we would do it in "Sea Runners," plastic boats that I believe to be at the top of the list of plastic boats.

As I continued to plan the trip it became evident that we most likely were going to have to spend at least a couple of nights out at sea. There were miles of coast where there were cliffs and no beaches. If we were forced to stay out all night, one of us could rest (it's impossible to sleep) while the other one maintained stability and direction. Doubles also had the advantage of letting one of us continue to paddle if the other one received an injury or became ill. The trip could continue. I also became aware of the fact that no one had ever paddled the entire west coast of Baja in a double kayak. We could be the first.

The two main drawbacks to using double kayaks are that they don't maneuver as well in the surf as singles do, and they don't hold as much gear as two singles do. We discussed it, and I changed my mind again and decided on doubles. How many times do you get to be first at anything?

Dave had a "Tofino" made by Necky. It was Kevlar but not made extra heavy for this kind of expedition. He and Jan did some fiberglass work on it and put extra stiffness across the underside of the deck. When they got through, the boat was much stronger than it was originally. I had Necky make a Tofino for me also. Because mine was made specifically for the expedition, it was constructed of double layered Kevlar top and bottom. It is heavy—ninety pounds—but as tough as they come. We had our boats.

Paddles were next for me. My seven foot, six inch paddle worked fine from the front seat of the boat but was a little short for the back position because the boat was several inches wider there. I had a special Kevlar paddle made by Lightning Paddles in Oregon. It is lighter than the normal glass paddle with a slightly larger blade. It is all one piece, stronger than the shaft that comes apart in the middle. I had my paddle made 'unfeathered,' which means the blades are on the same plane with each other. The reason I chose unfeathered paddles was that I expected the wind to be from the northwest ninety percent of the time. With the wind at our backs, the end of the paddle that is in the air would act as a sail and help us. The feathered or twisted paddle is only an advantage if the wind is blowing in your face. The other three settled on standard two piece paddles by Werner made out of fiberglass. My spare paddle would be a Werner also.

The next item to consider were the spray skirts. This is very important because it is the only thing that keeps your body and the ocean separated. It is the barrier that keeps every wave from filling your cockpit with water. Because of the extreme pressure placed on the spray skirt by pounding surf, I had Snapdragon of Seattle, Washington, make custom skirts for my boat. It takes two men and a boy to pull them off, but if we found ourselves flipped over I was sure I'd find the strength.

Other pieces of standard equipment to take are the P.F.D. (Personal Floatation Device), or life jacket, which would fold under my legs in the cockpit, the hand bilge pump, which fits beside my seat on the left side, along with a large sponge and a long sleeve paddle jacket. On the right side of my seat will be mounted the EPIRB (Emergency Position Indicating Radio Beacon). This is an emergency signaling device that sends a message into the air to be read by any commercial airlines, etc. When and if, weather permitting—we crossed to Cedros Island, we would be thirty miles from the closest land. The EPIRB just seemed like a good idea to me. After all, I'm fifty-seven, and that puts me past the age of immortality.

Behind my seat will be two gallons of water and a survival kit containing a fire starter, a space blanket, knife, etc. Between my legs will be the water maker. Our water maker is a reverse osmosis pump capable of making one quart of fresh water every fifteen minutes from salt water.

The only problem is that someone will have to pump it by hand. Not a hard task, but definitely energy consuming. We will have to pump at least two hours a day just to get two quarts each. That's not enough, but we hope to supplement our supply on occasion from land sources or passing yachts. We will have to be careful not to cut back on water just because we don't want to pump it. Proper hydration is absolutely essential to our well being.

We have a sail called a Vee Sail. It works well if the wind is behind you. Our prevailing winds should be northwest, which puts them behind us most of the time. The sail will be good for two main things. One is to help us rest when the wind comes up in the afternoon, and the second is to help us make speed when we get a strong wind. The wind should come up between 11 a.m. and 1 p.m. most every day and blow around ten to twenty knots. We will be in mid paddle about that time and can sail while we pump water. By late afternoon the seas will be too big to sail safely and we can paddle again. At least it looks good on paper. You'll have to read the log to see how it works out. If El Nino continues, we'll have weather right in our faces all the way down and the sails will be useless.

In order to use sails, we will have to have one for each boat so we can stay together. I bought one, tried it, and was pleased with the results. I ordered a second sail six weeks before our trip and sent a check to the manufacturer. He cashed my check but never sent the sail. I started calling two weeks before we left but only got a recorder each time I called. No one called back. My wife started sewing and I visited all the hardware stores in town and we made our own sail for $70.00 instead of the $300.00 to buy one. When I get back from the trip I'll go after my money. I don't like people that cheat me. [I discovered upon my return he was out of business and I never did recover my $300.00].

Our navigation gear will consist of a compass (and two spares), waterproof binoculars, an auto club map of Baja, a complete set of marine charts of the coast (laminated to keep them dry), and a set of topo maps of the entire coastline to help us find where we can come in at night. We also will have hand-held marine radios, mainly to talk to each other. If we get separated, which is very easy at night in high seas, the radios will help us locate one another again. The range of the radios from our low position in the kayak will be only about two miles.

I have written on one auto club map of Baja all the beach and coastal information I could get from reading off-road Baja books and magazine articles. The magazine Baja Explorer was a great help in several areas. Between charts, topos, and road maps we have a good idea where we are going.

I have driven the entire coast but at that time I didn't look at it from a kayaker's viewpoint so my recollections are, for the most part, of minimal value. It's too bad we can't look ahead in life to see where we are going. We could be so much better prepared when we get there.

In order to document the trip I will take slides and videos. This represents more of a challenge than I had expected. We will be wet most the time. Having taught photography at five different colleges and illustrated both the marine biology book and SCUBA book that I wrote, I know what I would like to do. The frustrating part is we won't have the room for the cameras.

I bought a good handy cam video and then ordered an underwater case for it. The plan was to carry it on deck and video as we went along. The manufacturer assured me the case would fit. When it arrived it didn't fit the camera. So now I have a video camera, which is very sensitive to moisture, in a kayak! I bought a Pelican waterproof case to carry it. I'll have to figure out how to use it during the trip.

For still camera equipment, I'm carrying a Nikon "Action Touch" camera in the cockpit with me. It is waterproof. I am also taking my Nikon 2000 in a waterproof carrying case to cover things on shore. These are excellent cameras and I should have a show of some kind when I return. I expect the other three will have cameras, too. Among the four of us we should do alright. I hope to have some good photos to include in this book.

Clothes always present a problem for me on any trip. They take up so much room and generally I only use half of what I take. Well, I've solved that problem. I'm only taking half of what I think I'll need. That way I should come out even.

As I write this my list consists of one pair of walking shorts, one pair of sandals, one T-Shirt, and one pair of clean undershorts. These will be kept in a dry bag until we get to Cabo. These are my dress up clothes. One ripstop nylon windbreaker, one fleece shirt, two t-shirts, one pair of gym shorts, one pair of paddle pants (a fairly heavy leotard-type pant) and a fleece cap are my dry clothes to wear in camp every night.

The rest of my clothes consist of one bathing suit, one long-sleeved white dress shirt (any old one will do) to wear while I paddle to keep the sun from cremating my body, two wide brim white canvas hats to keep the sun off my bald head, and two paddle jackets—a long-sleeved one for those cold mornings and stormy nights and a short sleeved one for general wind protection at chilly times. I will keep the long-sleeved shirt wet whenever it gets hot to inhibit my need to sweat and lose water. My paddle shoes and camp shoes will be the same pair of heavy soled water sandals. This collection may sound like a lot but what I'm not wearing will pack down into a small package.

Camp gear will make up a main part of our cargo. We will be out forty nights. My sleeping bag is a two and a half pound bag. It is not filled with down because down is useless when it gets damp. The sleeping bag fits into a Goretex bivy sack. A bivy sack is a thin bag to cover the sleeping bag and keep the wetness from dew or rain from soaking the sleeping camper during the night. The Goretex material keeps water out but lets sweat from the body evaporate so you don't get clammy in the bag. Inside the bivy sack and outside the sleeping bag I will slide a three quarter length therm-a-rest pad. This pad is in a canvas covering that snaps together to also serve as my chair. My eating utensils are a plastic spoon and fork, a large thermal cup, and a plastic plate.

We will take one windscreen and stove per boat. The stove in our boat is Glenn's and will burn any fuel we can find. The stove in the other boat runs on small butane cartridges. One large pot for stew and boiling water, one fry pan, and one small grill to place over an open fire comprises our cooking gear. We will also be taking a tepee style tent that Glenn has for mountaineering. It has a single center pole and no floor, but we can all get in it if we need to get out of the wind and cold. If the weather is good we won't need the tent, and we will sleep on the beach in our bivy sacks.

That brings us to food. We need to take all the good food we can carry. There are few towns within our reach from the water to resupply us. There are towns at Cedros, Bahia Tortugas, Punta Asuncion, Punta Abreojos, Bahia San Juanico, San Carlos and Todos Santos. There are also fish camps here and there along the way. Supplies of the type we are used to, however, will not be available. We will be able to get tortillas, which are important as a carbohydrate source, some fruit, some vegetables, some types of cheese, and refried beans—all good stuff, but not as complete as we need to paddle ten hours a day. We will take with us a lot of powdered and dehydrated food.

We can use things like power bars, dried fruit and nuts to give us fuel to burn during the day by eating a small amount every hour. It is important to maintain proper glucose levels. Electrolyte replacement to put in the water we drink during the day to keep our sodium and potassium levels up is a must. We also will take some highly nutritious powdered food to mix in with our other food to insure a complete balance of amino acids and minerals. I will also be taking a vitamin packet each day as a type of insurance against any deficiency in our diet. If we can maintain good nutrition, we should get stronger as we go. If we get weaker, we will slow down because we will have to rest more. [As I write this our starting date is only four weeks off and El Nino is still blowing winds from the south. If that doesn't change soon we may be getting more rest than we want.]

The food I am packing is being stored for the most part in the mylar bags I saved out of the boxes of wine I bought at my local store. Drink the wine and save the bag inside. It makes getting ready for the trip worthwhile. These bags are so strong that I blew one up and sat on it. I weigh two hundred thirty pounds. It held fine. I take the spout off by taking the edge of it in my teeth and pulling it right off. I wash the bag, hold a hair dryer so the hot air circulates into the bag to dry it out, and then I have a gallon container that gets smaller as I use it. (I just suck the air out.) It is tough and totally waterproof. Even if the trip doesn't turn out well, it will be worth it just to have had all the enjoyment of collecting my thirteen bags.

In two bags I have a breakfast mix that is composed of instant oatmeal, oat bran, instant cream of wheat, powdered milk, and sugar. I have used this mixture for years on my survival class field trips. My students have named it 'John slop.' To use it, we fill a cup one-third full of the mixture and then fill the cup with boiling water. Stir and wait five minutes—a great breakfast. A second cup can be made using a little more of the powder and a little less water. It will gel in ten minutes and can be carried in a closed cap thermos cup to be eaten during a rest stop or for lunch. Good complex carbohydrates. If that menu sounds a little monotonous remember we will only be out for forty days.

The contents of the other bags will be: one full of hot chocolate mix, one of instant potatoes, one of instant rice, and one of dehydrated mixed vegetables. (Did you know that the one pound mixed vegetable packets you buy frozen in the store dehydrate very well? Five of these big packages dehydrated into one small sandwich bag that weighs only a couple of ounces.) We also had one bag of almonds, and one bag of dehydrated fruit. (The dried fruit you buy in the store is generally not dry enough. One day in the dryer and it wasn't sticky any more.) One bag of macaroni, one bag of Top Ramen smashed up so it will go into the bag, one bag of powdered concentrated sports food, a couple of large blocks of cheese, a bag of tortilla mix, and perhaps a bag of pancake mix should just about do it. That's thirteen bags.

Seven full bags will fit in a long slender dry bag that fits between my legs in the cockpit. The others are stuffed wherever there is room because they can conform to any shape and are waterproof.

To supplement our food supply we will fish, dive, and scrounge from the tide pools. Glenn and Dave are taking rubber suits (the water is cold most of the way down) and skin diving gear. If I taught Glenn well, we'll eat fish. About now you're asking why, if I'm the diving instructor, don't I dive? The answer is simple. I figure after ten hours a day of paddling, my body is going to need all the rest it can get. I really don't mind getting old, in fact I really am enjoying it. But I sure do miss my younger body. Someone once said, "Pain builds character." If this is true I have built more character since I turned fifty than I can handle.

I plan to trail a fishing line behind the boat most every day. We should catch enough fish on the line so Glenn and Dave can rest if they want to. The tide pools are full of good food also. Limpets, mussels, and snails could give us all the protein we need.

Finally, I need a few personal items—comb, toothbrush, notebook, etc. I'm carrying a small mini-cassette tape recorder to keep the log. I figure I'll be too tired to write much, but an old school teacher is never too tired to talk a lot.

GETTING IN SHAPE

Physically getting in shape has been the component of the expedition that has worried me the most. There are many ways to walk the edge in life, and pushing your physical ability is just one of them. I have pushed my physical ability before in athletic competitions so I understand the kind of commitment it takes. I pushed to make it to the olympic trials in cycling in 1960. I pushed to take a third place in the Western United States Judo Championships in 1956. I have not, however, been in the position where if I didn't push enough it would have made any difference except to my ego. This time it is different.

If I break down physically during the Baja expedition, I will endanger my life and the lives of three others. Compound that fact with the second fact that neither I nor any of the other three, have ever tried an ultra-endurance activity before, we have no track record to base probabilities on. These two factors have given me enough motivation and concern to get in the best physical shape this old body can attain.

When I retired in May of 1991, I had not been working out physically other than the cycling I did three times a week with a friend. For thirteen years I had been riding my bike along the bike path from Newport Beach to Long Beach, California, and back most Monday, Wednesday and Friday mornings. The rides were twenty-five to fifty miles depending on my work schedule and we averaged fifteen miles per hour. This was just the right amount of exercise to keep me healthy but certainly not enough to keep me in shape. I am six feet tall and when I retired I weighed two hundred thirty-five pounds, had a forty-one inch waist and a forty-four inch chest. If I were to be considered in shape for anything at that time it would have been Sumo wrestling. Our departure date was May 16, 1992. I had one year to make some changes.

I bought a Concept II Rowing Machine and started a cross training program of exercise. I started out by rowing one thousand meters, then jogging a half mile, rowing one thousand meters and jogging another half mile. I didn't want to put too much stress on any one part of my body for any extended period of time to start. I would repeat this cycle of row—run—row—run until I got tired. Starting out it was about five or six cycles. I did this four times a week.

After a month, the cycle had increased to two thousand meters and one mile and I had added one of the spring exercisers to my program. It was a device like I used to see in the ads where the big guy kicked sand in the little guy's face. It had two handles connected by five springs. I couldn't pull it. I took off one of the springs. I still couldn't pull it. I took off two, then three, and I could finally pull it. I included a series of exercises that I would just struggle to do ten times. As the time passed I could do fifteen and then twenty. At that point I put the third spring back on. When I got to twenty with three springs (I was still jogging and rowing), it was time to add to the workout.

I bought a weight bench with a bunch of odds and ends attached to it. I added bench presses, "lat" curls, "quad" curls, hamstring curls, biceps curls and situps to my program. I started with one set of each and built up over a couple of months to three sets each. I also got out at least once a week for an eight to ten mile paddle during that period, but the general strength and endurance training was a higher priority than paddling to start with. A friend came by at the end of one of my harder workouts when I could hardly stand up and was having difficulty talking. He asked me, "aren't you a little old for this?"

"I don't think so," I wheezed back at him.

"How will you know when you're too old?" he asked.

"When it takes me longer to urinate than it does to have sex I'll be too old," I answered.

In February 1992 I started paddling more and increased my miles per month from the fifty to seventy that I had been doing for eight months to one hundred seventy per month. In March and April I changed the entire workout to mainly paddling.

My kayak is in the water in the Port Ludlow, Washington marina where I have a slip for another boat I own. My routine was now to run to the marina, which is one half mile, paddle as hard as I could for three to five hours and then run home. I averaged four and one-half knots which is a good steady pace. I'm using a heavy paddle and porgies which are rubber hand protectors so my hands wouldn't freeze off. The porgies are quite heavy and add to the exercise program. Some mornings there has been ice all over my kayak when I get to it at 6 a.m. These are the times I wonder, "What the hell am I doing?"

Now the big question. Has all this pain, suffering and sweat done any good? Yes, it has. When I started I would work out for one hour and sleep for six. Now I can work out hard for six hours and go on with my other daily chores and not be tired. I am fully rested after about six hours of sleep instead of the eight I once needed, and I feel much better.

I did a lean body tissue test when I started. That's a bad test that tells you what percent of your body is ugly fat. Remember—I said my weight was two hundred thirty-five pounds and my waist was forty-one inches. Well, my percent of fat was twenty-six. That meant that only one hundred seventy-four pounds of my two hundred thirty-five pounds was muscle, and sixty-one pounds of me was soft, greasy fat. The only word for that is obese. Now in April, eleven months later, my weight is two hundred twenty-six, my waist is thirty-nine inches and my percent fat is twenty. I am now one hundred eighty-one pounds muscle and only forty-five pounds of ugly fat. That is sixteen pounds less for me to carry around.

I have not tried to lose weight because I believe I will lose quite a bit on the trip and the extra fat I start with will be a help to maintain energy during the paddle. My chest measurement has gone from forty-four inches to forty-nine inches from the weight training and paddling. All in all I've done the best I could without totally dedicating my life to it.

My wife told me she will be so happy when this obsession is over. It has preoccupied me day and night. I have thought so much about the "what ifs" that I think I have most of them covered, and I have trained hard enough that I should be able to hold together physically. The actual trip may be anticlimactic. Whatever happens on the trip I have had one full year of excitement already. All that's left now is to "just do it."

Prologue

It is June 19, 1992. I am sitting in my chair on the sand at Lover's Beach, in Cabo San Lucas. We have completed the paddle. My three compadres left on the 4:30 p.m. bus for Tijuana. They will arrive there at 4:30 p.m. tomorrow. A short taxi ride to the border, a train ride to the Santa Ana station in California and their expedition is over. From what I hear about the Baja buses the most dangerous and exciting part of the entire journey may be the next twenty-four hours for them.

We arrived on the beach at Cabo San Lucas at 1:18 p.m. on June 18, 1992. Our total time from Shelter Island, San Diego, California, to Cabo San Lucas was thirty-three days, four hours and eighteen minutes. It feels good to be the first to do something. Although Ed Gillet and paddling partner Steve Landick made the same journey in 1982, they did it in singles—we did it in doubles, and we did it faster.

Sitting here in the hot Baja sun on a beach crammed with tourists from the cruise ships in the harbor and all the people from town brought out here by pongas, I am experiencing a limbo of feelings.

If I had not been in Cabo in 1969 and 1970, I would probably like it. I remember it as a sleepy little village of about five hundred people. All of them were nice and, generally, interested in talking to me. Now it is all big hotels full of gringos wearing shorts, Hawaiian shirts, and black socks. One such individual, when told to "be careful of the urchins," took the cigar out of his mouth and replied, "Urchins, urchins, what the hell is an urchin? I thought these waters were safe!" The real Mexican town still exists, more or less, in back of the hustle and bustle of the main city. It is kind of an "across the tracks" section. Too bad the tourist never sees it. It is the real Cabo San Lucas.

For thirty-three days we have camped on isolated beaches with no human traffic of any kind. Pigs rooted us in our sleeping bags, mice bit our fingers while we slept. Coyotes chewed up our dive gear, crabs crawled over our face at night, and no food of any kind, in any container, was safe from the rats. I cursed all these critters as each one entered my life, but I would go back to any one of those beaches to get away from the swarming humans on this beach.

If you are one of the people that love it the way it is now, just consider the source of the above comments. I'm a crotchety old fart who probably doesn't know what he's talking about anyway. One of the tourists walked up to me today and said, "Don't you just love it? It gets better and better every year."

Before I could answer, his wife said, "My three ex-husbands never took me to places like this."

Then turning to her husband, she said, "Walk out in the water with me so I don't get knocked on my can while I pee." At least some people still love it here.

For the next three days I must camp here and wait for my wife, Sharon, to arrive by car and carry me away to a safe haven in Washington state where we live. I have lots of time to kill waiting so I have decided to spend some of it videotaping the goings-on here on the beach. I am sure it will be almost as funny as a good Goldie Hawn movie. I'll watch it on a cold winter night in Washington when I am wishing I was some place warmer. It will help to squelch any urge I may have to come back to Cabo San Lucas. I still love Baja. I just don't love tourists, even though down here I am one.

I kept a daily log of the trip and will do my best to tell you our story. The log will reflect only the way I saw the trip. The four of us never really talked about how we were feeling about things. I guess men just don't share their inner feelings easily, even with close friends. I think we all felt somewhat the same as we were standing in the street of Cabo shaking hands and saying goodbye. I really cared for those guys, but all I said was, "It was a good trip." I felt a great loss as they walked away to the bus station and I limped back to the boat on my bad foot to paddle back to Lover's Beach and wait for Sharon.

By six o'clock all the tourists had been taken back to their hotels by the water taxis and I was alone on the beach. The one burner stove was hissing away heating the water for my Top Ramen dinner. I ate my noodles, drank a cup of hot chocolate, and looked up at the moon. I wondered, "what do you do after you've walked on the moon?" The best answer I could come up with was to take a walk on the beach. So I did. In the warm evening I felt a heavy loneliness. I missed my wife, and my three friends. My mind drifted back to day one.....

Week One

DAY 1—MAY 16, 1992

Sharon and I stay at the Point Loma Inn the night before we are to leave. We leave a wake up call for 5:30 a.m. so we can get our gear together and meet some family and friends for breakfast at Denny's at 7 a.m. Our friends, Ted and Marge Dieterich, do the same thing. The people at the motel never do give us a wake-up call. Fortunately, we wake up in time without their help, but I won't stay there again. Their irresponsibility could have caused some real problems with our schedule.

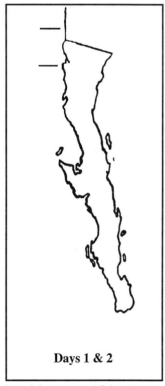

Days 1 & 2

We have breakfast at Denny's with twenty friends and family members and then go to the beach at Shelter Island. Ed and Katie Gillet have kept our boats for us at their shop, "Southwest Sea Kayaking," and bring them to us on their kayak trailer. Ed also gives us a small emergency beacon to use instead of the larger one I had purchased for the trip.

The smaller one saves us both weight and space. Ed holds the record for the longest unassisted kayak adventure in the world, from the coast of California to Hawaii. He has been a teacher and inspiration to me and hundreds of others.

There are more people on the beach than I had expected. After we leave the beach I realize I was so hyper with the packing of the boat that I hardly said hello to a number of good friends and family that came a long way to see us off, and I feel very bad about that. I hope they understand my mental anxiety and preoccupation at that particular time and forgive me.

Jan says, "If they cared enough to come down, they care enough to understand." I feel better because I realize he is right.

It is said that every good story has many parts. One of the unusual parts of our story was quite tragic and unexpected. I had a cousin, Judy Reseck who lived in the Escondido area (near San Diego, California). About four weeks before we were to leave she wrote me a wonderful encouraging letter about the trip. She was planning to come down to see us off. When I arrived in California from Washington, I called to tell her where to meet us. Her husband answered the phone and told me, "We lost Mother yesterday." She had passed away the day before Mother's Day. He said they were going to have her ashes spread at sea. I told him she had been so excited about our trip it would be an honor for me to take her ashes out to sea with us as we left on our adventure. He agreed she would have liked that and it was set.

Judy's family brought her ashes to me at the beach and she joins us as we start our adventure. Something happens I don't expect.

The other three ask, "Who was she?" I tell them about her as we paddle out of San Diego harbor, expecting to spread her ashes when we get into open ocean. Jan says, "I think she ought to make the whole trip with us." It is agreed upon, and Judy Reseck becomes a member of the crew for the entire Baja trip. She would have loved it. Who knows—maybe she did!

We are concerned about the boat traffic in the harbor as we leave. When we set the date of May 16 we chose it because it was a good weather time of the year to start. What we didn't know was that it would also end up being the last and deciding day of the America's Cup Race in San Diego. Navy ships are cruising all over the place and an aircraft carrier almost runs us down outside the harbor. A patrol boat comes up to us and asks us to keep clear of the harbor. We tell him we are heading south and we paddle faster.

We paddle for four hours and the wind comes up so we decide to try our sails. I have the commercial sail and the other boat has the sail my wife and I made. Getting the sails up the first time is like a Laurel and Hardy movie because Jan and Dave have never used one. Glenn and I had a little practice beforehand on a trial paddle we took to Catalina Island and back. After a lot of naughty words, lost tempers, and looks of aggression we are all under sail. The wind holds for three hours and we decide to find a place to come in and spend the night. We take down the sails and start paddling just behind the breaker line looking for a suitable spot to get through the surf and camp. It is difficult along here because most of the places we can land are private. Two hours later we find a spot under the sand dunes just north of the Half Way House. We realize as we scope it out we have to be careful because they run ATV's (All Terrain Vehicles) up and down the dune and we don't want to get run over while we sleep.

The surf line is extensive, starting off the beach about eighty yards, but not very big, only three to four feet high. Should be no problem.

Everything goes smoothly. Glenn and I come in on the back of one large swell and stroke it for the beach. The next one breaks and catches us with three feet of whitewater—no problem. Turn sideways, go into a broach and let the wave push you along in front of it. Brace by holding the paddle out under the wave so you don't tip over, and ride it out. From the back position I push down on the paddle and the boat straightens out as the wave pushes the bow around and we stick our nose on the beach. We do it just fine. Better than fine—we are great. We are in the process of telling each other how great we are when Jan yells at us, "Get the bag."

What we don't realize is the net bag strapped to the stern of our boat has been ripped off by the force of the wave. Dave and Jan come in behind us and, luckily, see it rip off. When they hit the beach Jan runs out into the surf and grabs the bag. In it is all of Glenn's dive gear. We stop congratulating each other and realize we have almost blown it.

As we start to unpack the boats to make them light enough for us to lift up the beach for the night, we realize we have also lost one half of the spare paddle we had tied on the back. It had been tied partly to the bag and the bag took the paddle with it when it left. One half a paddle was fine as a spare because we could use it canoe style if we had to. The bad part is that this was no ordinary paddle. We had borrowed it at the last minute from Ed Gillet because we forgot to bring ours. It isn't just a paddle, it is the one he had taken on his miraculous Hawaiian passage. We are stunned when we realize we have lost it. We all go into the water and comb the area for half an hour. No luck. We are all depressed.

We set up camp and cook up eight Top Ramen's for dinner. We have covered thirty-seven miles in ten hours. It has been a good day except for the lost paddle. Everyone is very quiet. I wonder if it is because we are tired or depressed about the paddle. I decide it is the paddle. We're not that tired, but we are ready to sleep. The trip is under way.

DAY 2—MAY 17, 1992

We are up at first light and pack our gear back in the dry bags. Glenn has become our camp cook because he is the only one that can make his blow-torch of a stove work. He has the water boiling in minutes and we are ready for the oatmeal mix we will devour for breakfast. We must be really hungry—it actually tastes good.

The tide is very low and we walk a mile of beach looking for the lost paddle. Jan walks the water's edge while the rest of us search higher on the beach. No luck. We had hoped it might wash up on the beach during the night when the tide came in.

We carry the boats down to the water and repack them. We are off the beach by 7 a.m. and get our faces washed by the waves on the way out, but have no real problems. Being soaking wet makes us cold and gives us good motivation to paddle harder to get warm.

The day is still and semi-foggy. Our visibility is only about two miles. We stay along the shore for awhile then decide to use the compass and head off shore. We set a course into the fog for Todos Santos Island. After a couple of hours we get nervous. It is a longer paddle than we thought. We are only out for seven hours and twenty minutes, but in the fog where we can see nothing but each other. It seems to take forever. We do our twenty-five miles and hit the island dead on. The fog always makes me nervous, even in a big boat, but at least we know our compass is accurate.

Todos Santos Island (a composite of two islands) has a good landing spot on the north side of the south island. It is a rock beach but protected from the surf and easy to land on. We set up camp—which means we unload the boats enough so we can lift them above high tide line. We have to lift the boats and carry them because if we drag them, which would be easier, we would tear out the bottoms on the rocks or wear through it in the sand. With four of us to lift it isn't too bad even over the uneven slippery rocks.

Dave and Glenn get out their dive gear and go after dinner. Jan and I start pumping fresh water through our reverse osmosis pump. In an hour we have a gallon. The divers return with five small fish. They take over the pump and produce another gallon of fresh water. Just as we are putting away the fresh water pump, two single kayaks come around the corner. A young couple introduce themselves as Brian and Andromeda from Nova Scotia, Canada. They had paddled for four months on the inside of the Sea of Cortez and were now trying the outside of Baja. They are novice boaters and thought ten miles a day to be almost extreme. They share some fun stories with us about their adventure.

Andromeda says she is a professional writer and is writing a guide to kayaking in Baja. Somehow the conversation got around to getting back into your boat if you capsize. She says, "We tried that, but it was too hard." We gently express the opinion that it is an important skill which everyone needs to have to be safe.

She tells us, "There seems to be two schools of thought on that—one that thinks self-rescues are important and one that says just be careful and don't fall out of your boat." There really isn't any more for us to say. I was real proud of all of us for our restraint. (We do, however, during the rest of our trip, keep reminding each other what school of thought we should belong to. On several occasions we obviously forget because Glenn and I capsize once and Jan and Dave capsize twice. I guess Glenn and I have a better memory.)

Andromeda is fascinated by my mylar bags that our food is stored in. I tell her, "They are wine containers."

She asks if she can tell about them in her book if she gives me credit.

I say, "Of course." (I believe in giving credit where credit is due, and I would love to know who told her about the "two schools of thought," so I could give that person the credit he deserves for endangering the lives of two very nice people).

For dinner we have the first fish of the trip and our Top Ramen.

Jan and Dave elect to sleep on the rock beach next to the boats and Glenn and I choose to sleep up on the bluff in the bird crap. Our two new friends sleep in their tent on the bluff. It is cold, damp, and windy. It feels good. All is well with the world.

DAY 3—MAY 18, 1992

The morning is overcast and heavy with haze. We decide because of our long first day we will only go eighteen miles today. That will keep us on schedule and will take us to Puerto Santo Tomas. We leave the beach at 7 a.m. and paddle six hours to get there. A very strong wind comes up just as we arrive. With no reason to stop we decide to try the sails again and make a few more miles. We get the sails up and the boats jump to near eight knots. We have visions of making many miles. After five minutes the sail is ripped out of Glenn's hands by a huge gust of wind and hits the water where it breaks in half. I hear Glenn say something like, "Oh poo poo." Our sailing is over for awhile.

We fold and stow the sails in the cockpits and land on a sand beach through a stiff surf. The rudder on our boat is bent at a right angle as a wave crashes on it. We start to wonder about the trip. Only three nights out and we have lost our extra paddle, broken our sail, lost one hat in the surf, and bent our rudder. Oh well, as the bumper sticker so aptly states, "shit happens!"

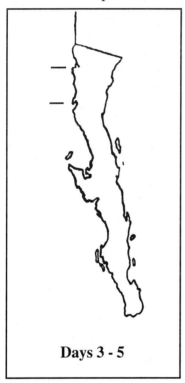

Days 3 - 5

We fix the sail by using a section of our tent pole as a sleeve to slip over the broken stay. We are lucky, it fits. We fix the rudder by taking it off the boat and beating it between two boulders on the beach. By the time the sun goes down we are ready again. We eat our Top Ramen and crawl into our bivey sacks to get rested for tomorrow. The wind blows all night but we use our boats as wind breaks and sleep well.

DAY 4—MAY 19, 1992

The sun is our alarm clock. We start packing the boats at first light. Glenn gets the stove going and heats water for our gruel. We eat breakfast out of our cups and get off the beach at 7:10 a.m. Our goal today is Puerto San Isidro, twenty-five miles south. After we have paddled three hours a strong wind comes up rather suddenly and we try our mended sail. We sail for two hours and make it to San Isidro. The repaired sail works like new.

We buy some supplies (sodas, Snickers bars and tortillas) and send a message home through two fishermen on their way back to the states. They say they will call and give our location to Sharon.

It soon became evident that the entire success or failure of the expedition depended on our ability to repair everything we brought with us.

The wind is still in the right direction when we finish our shopping so we climb back in our boats and sail five miles farther down the coast. The sail in our boat is a bit larger than the sail in Dave's boat. Jan has to paddle along with Dave holding the sail to keep up with us. We start looking for a place to come in.

The surf is four feet with sets of six to seven footers sneaking in every now and then. We find a big rock just a hundred feet off shore and Glenn and I shoot in behind it. One heavy broach and we are washed up on the sand.

While Dave and Jan are watching us go in, one big sucker of a wave they don't see sneaks up and grabs them from behind. We look up just in time to see them get caught. It is gorgeous. Their stern lifts high in the air. They realize they are had. Their eyes get big as saucers. The boat shoots down the wave before they can broach it. The bow is driven deep into the water and hits the sand. The stern goes straight over the top. End-over-end in a twenty foot boat is something to see.

The next twenty minutes is spent chasing gear in the surf and bailing out a boat that now, because of the shock of being driven into the sand, has lost its watertight bulkheads. We also remind them several times they have forgotten which "school of thought" they are supposed to belong to.

The gear is laid out and gets almost dry. The bulkheads are resealed with silicon, and we are ready again. While their gear is drying I am tending to seven quarter sized boils that have formed on the outside of my left leg where it rubs against the hull. I scrub them with soap and fresh water. All I can do is let them come to a head and drain. I have never had boils before and boy, do they hurt. To avoid further problems I adjust my gear so my legs will not rub on it constantly, and start wearing polypropolene bicycle pants for protection. *(The boils go away in a week and I'm not bothered by them again).*

As we eat our Top Ramen the decision is made to make it to San Martin Island tomorrow. We have come thirty miles today and there appears to be no good landing spot on the coast for many more miles. The shoreline consists of big surf and steep beaches—a bad combination. We don't need another end-over.

Sand is blowing in a strong wind and taking pictures without getting sand in the cameras is impossible. It looks like the rest of the trip is going to be plagued by blowing sand. The sand is so fine it is almost like powder. We give it a name: microsand. That sounds better than what we were calling it at first. I won't mention what that was because my grandchildren may read this book.

This venture is becoming a series of problems to solve. We start believing, "the only good day is yesterday." It's the only day we can be sure we are going to make it through.

DAY 5—MAY 20, 1992

We get up at daylight to find a beautiful day. No wind and lots of sunshine. Glenn has the pot boiling before we can even carry our gear down to the water. We eat our "John Slop" as usual and carry the rest of the gear down to the water's edge. Next the boats are placed as far into the surf as possible without being carried away and we start the morning "stuffing ritual." Each of us is responsible for packing the same equipment in the same place in the boat each morning. By having a fixed ritual the packing goes fast and we don't forget anything.

As we are stuffing our gear into the boat, a little larger set of waves roll up higher on the beach, moving the boats around. We grab them and hold the bows out so the water doesn't splash into the cockpit flooding the boats. We mutter a few choice words but don't pay much attention to what has just happened. A bad mistake for Glenn and me.

The boats are now full and sealed up. We are ready to launch. Dave and Jan are the first out. We watch the surf and give them a push off the beach when it flattens out between sets. We watch as they punch through a couple of three foot waves. Once behind the surf break they turn their bow towards shore to watch us come out.

Glenn and I seal up our spray skirts and wait for the water to come up higher on the beach and float our boat so we can paddle out. We know the water will come and get us because it came up that far on the beach when we were loading the boats. What we hadn't taken time to ask ourselves is, "Why did the water come up higher?" We were too preoccupied with the trivia of loading and keeping the boats stable to ask such an obvious question. The answer, of course, is flagrantly evident. The water comes up higher on the beach when the waves are bigger. The next bit of information which we understand, but fail to apply, is that bigger waves as a rule come in sets of six to twelve. It, therefore, is only logical that if you sit on the sand and wait for a larger than normal wave to wash you off the beach, it will be the first of a larger than normal set. Some very smart person once told me, "If you have a dumb head, your whole body suffers." He was right. A giant wave shoots up the beach and sucks us out. We paddle as hard as we can. The whole object of this game is to spend as little time as possible in the surf zone.

I hear Glenn say, "Oh shit!" I tilt my head back so I can see from under the broad brim of my "official life guard hat" and find three five-foot walls of water racing each other to see who can eat us first. Glenn disappears under the foam about ten milliseconds before I do. My memory is not too good after that but I remember how surprised I am when we pop out of the foam and are still upright and paddling. There is just enough time to gulp in a breath of air and under we go again.

Out we pop—"paddle! paddle!" I scream.

"What the hell do you think I'm doing?" comes a voice from somewhere under the foam of the next wave.

Out again, breath—under—out—breath—under. This goes on for six minutes. Eleven walls of white water. We make it through. I feel like we have just finished our twenty-five miles for the day. I am panting for air and at the same time shouting "All right!"

Glenn says, "My hat! Damn it, I lost my hat. That was my best hat. It's been everywhere with me for years." He is really upset. For a minute I think we are going back to look for it.

Then he calms down and says, "Screw it." We are back to normal.

We paddle for three hours. A light wind comes up so we break out the sails and sail for three and half more hours. It looks like we can make San Martin Island before dark with this wind, so we change our course off shore on a heading to the island. The weather is overcast and we are depending on our compass course. As soon as we get well offshore the wind, of course, dies and the water gets dead calm. We are now committed to a much longer paddle than we had planned. We started our paddle about five miles south of San Isedro, and San Martin is better than fifty miles down the coast. Our plan was to sail most of it but that just isn't going to happen. We are able to sail about twelve miles before the wind dies but the rest is going to be up to the internal combustion engine commonly called the human body. We eat all the food we have on deck and start paddling.

Paddling on a dead calm sea in a haze where nothing is visible under a heavy overcast sky is boring. Hour after hour drift by; only our faith tells us we are moving. At 7:30, just before it gets dark, we are just able to make out the island. In the hazy conditions it still looks a long way from us. The wind starts to build and soon is up to fifteen knots. The water is white capping but now it is dark and we can't sail in the dark and stay together. We keep paddling.

The dark that surrounds us is tomb-like. With the heavy marine overcast, not even a hint of the moon or a star is visible. We have two small strobe lights. They are water proof and run for seventeen hours on one 'D' size battery. We put one on the stern of each boat. In the total blackness these little strobes are blinding. We have to keep them on so we don't get separated, but we have to be careful not to look at them. When they flash it is like someone discharging a camera flash in your face. We do the best we can to keep the boats even so the lights are behind both of us. It is becoming increasingly more difficult to do as the seas get larger.

The wind is building and there are whitecaps that break over the stern on to my back every now and then. We consider sailing again, but don't feel it is safe to sail in this blackness because if a boat capsizes its strobe light will be under water and out of sight and the other boat will lose contact instantly. By the time the second boat got its sail down it would be very difficult, if not impossible, to turn around and find the capsized boat in the dark and rough seas.

We can see a small light ahead. We don't know what it is but it's on our course so we use it as a point to head for. The light helps a great deal because now we don't have to use a flashlight to read the compass. When we reach the light an hour later, we are pleased to find it is the anchor light of a large sail boat. We have to be in Hassler's Cove on San Martin Island. It is the only good anchorage anywhere around. It is 9:30 p.m.

We yell, "Hello." A lady comes out on deck.

"Can you tell us where you are anchored?" we ask.

"We're at San Martin Island," she replies, a bit confused at the question.

"Where on San Martin?," we ask.

She confers with someone inside and says, "Hassler's Cove." We ask, "Can you tell us where the beach is?" Hassler's Cove is created by a natural rock jetty that is under water at high tide and has many jagged rocks right at the surface. We don't want to get involved with the surf breaking on the rocks in this blackout. We know there is a sand beach a hundred yards or so long in the cove because we've all, except Glenn, been there before.

The lady says, "Just a minute." She goes below and gets a big light to shine on shore. We still can't see the beach but all of the yelling back and forth has caught the attention of some Mexican fishermen on shore. They have come down to the beach to see what the funny flashing lights are (not exactly standard running lights).

We see their flash lights on the beach and say, "Thank you," to the lady and shoot for shore before the lights go out.

We hit the beach before we see it. Glenn jumps out and I try to tell my body it is okay to move again. It takes a few seconds to wake it up so it can hear me, and then I get out too. There are definitely times I miss my youth!

The fishermen see we are soaking wet, cold, and tired. All of these things they understand as well as anyone can. Their entire lives they are wet, cold, and tired. They build a fire while we drag our boats above high water line for the night. We are too tired to lift them. Soon they have us warm by a large bonfire. They also make coffee to help us warm up. They ask in Spanish, "Where did you come from?"

We say, "San Diego."

They ask, "Where are you going?"

We say, "Cabo San Lucas."

They ask, "How many days?"

We say, "Forty."

They shake their heads, say something to each other we don't understand, and go to bed. We make some Top Ramen, and go to bed ourselves. We have been in the boats for over thirteen hours and have covered fifty-two miles. Some would consider that a good day. Others would consider it a dumb one. As I go to bed I am of the second opinion. In the morning I will probably be of the first one. After all we have already decided that yesterday was always a good day.

DAY 6—MAY 21, 1992

We are a full day ahead of schedule, so we decide to take it easy and only go as far as Rancho Soccoro, twenty miles down the coast. The water is flat calm and there is a heavy overcast sky. Jan complains about the lack of sun so

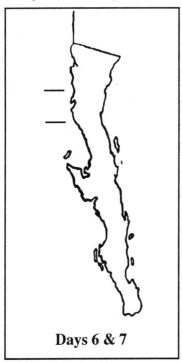

Days 6 & 7

far on the trip. He says he is "solar powered" and is about to run down. We see some Americans fishing from a sixteen foot Boston Whaler boat about a mile offshore and ask them to call Sharon to say we are still okay. They are a bit surprised as we paddle up and ask them for the favor, but write the phone number down on the inside flap of a book of matches. They say they will call in a few days when they get back to San Diego. We paddle for six more hours and arrive at Rancho Soccoro about 3:00 p.m. We can see sand beach in both directions for miles.

It all looks like an easy landing so we can go in anywhere. We decide to come in at the end of the sand dune where the homes are. Normally we would pick an isolated beach, but we need water and, rather than spend several hours pumping it, we will try to find a source to fill our containers in the settlement. It is high tide and the surf is in the four foot range. We come in fine, broach twice and straighten out to slide up on the beach when the boat hits and bounces off of something. We wash over it and climb out on shore. "What the hell was that?" I ask.

"Rocks," says Jan. "There are rocks all through the surf." What we didn't know was there had been a flood that winter and we are at the mouth of a normally dry river where it dumps into the ocean. As the tide recedes we realize we have just skimmed over acres of large boulders that had washed down with the flood. In the morning when the tide will be really low we will most likely have a problem getting out. We'll solve that problem in the morning. Right now we are on the beach safe and sound. We turn our attention to a more timely problem: Water.

We walk to the first house on the beach and ask if water is available. The man says, "Yes, we have a filtration unit, take all you need." We take all we have containers for, twelve and one-half gallons. While the young ones are filling up the water containers, the old one, me, is invited into the trailer to have a beer with our host.

"Buzz, is what they call me."

"My name's John, glad to meet you." We visit for about an hour which is how long it took his filtration system to produce twelve and one-half gallons of water. Buzz tells me about the flood that ran four feet deep down the canyon right over his car and washed out eighty feet of cement brick wall. That explains where all the rocks we landed over came from—down the canyon from the mountains. When we leave Buzz's we take the water plus two loaves of bread, eighteen eggs, twelve sausages, a half gallon of milk and several sodas with us. All are gifts from Buzz, our new friend.

As we shake hands goodbye, he says, "All the beach and roads down to the beach washed out during the flood. Now I won't have to put up with the RV'ers camping right in front of my place. There's no place out there left for them to park."

We thank him for his help and go back to our camp with all of our treasures. Boy, do we have a feast tonight! We have no way to save anything so we eat the food all at once. It is a great meal and is completely unexpected, which makes it taste even better.

One of the things I am really pleased about is how everyone is getting along. For a group that really didn't know each other before we started, you would think we have all been best friends for twenty years. Everyone is sensitive to what needs to be done without being asked. No one complains about or blames anyone else for anything. Everyone is ready to accept responsibility for himself and seems to have unlimited tolerance for the others. I will, of course, take credit for all of that because I'm the one that chose them. What a fantastic judge of people I am!

The other thing I am very pleased about is how well we are able to fix everything that breaks. I have a sense of well being about the trip now that I didn't have when we started. I believe we have been tested on enough occasions and in enough different ways to prove we can come through with flying colors. I feel we can handle it now, whatever it is. We truly have the focused strength of four whenever it is needed, and I am confident together we are more than adequate.

We decide to put the tent up because it looks like it is going to rain. The tent only has one center pole, and we had used a section of it to fix the broken sail a few days before, so we use the whole sail as the center pole. It works fine. It doesn't rain, but the dampness soaks everything anyway.

We have time to sit and talk as we finish our great meal. I want to get the feeling of the group about making the crossing to Cedros Island. If we decide to cross to Cedros at the north end we can save two or three days of paddling. We also will bypass a hundred miles of high impact surf along Malarrimo Beach and the Guerrero Negro Barrier Island, and we won't have to come back into the wind and head into the seas for fifty miles to make it around Punta Eugenia either. Any one of these reasons seemed good enough for me to make the fifty mile crossing when I was at home sitting at my dinner table drawing lines on the charts, but my attitude has changed. The main reason is the one and a half hours we had spent paddling in total darkness the day before. I didn't like it. I had been beyond my comfort zone farther than I want to admit. I had seen waves I braced for that didn't exist and I was caught not bracing for ones I didn't (couldn't) see. The water had been mild white caps (two and one-half to three foot seas), and during the Cedros crossing it could be five times rougher and just as dark. The heavy marine layer is still with us and every night is like being in a cave.

Our shortest distance from the mainland to the island is fifty miles and that course will put the prevailing wind directly on our starboard or right side. If the seas get as rough as they normally do, we might be forced to turn to port and angle down them. In the worst scenario, we could get blown down the east side of the island and miss it altogether only to be forced to land after a very long paddle of ninety to one hundred miles inside Punta Eugenia. We would be in total darkness for at least one entire night. I don't like any of it.

The second choice we have is to start the paddle from Isla Geronimo. This would be a ninety mile crossing but would put the wind and seas behind us where we can handle some pretty big stuff and still make the island. At best this would be a long paddle with at least nine hours of it in total darkness after we had already been paddling for ten hours or so—not a good place to be in high seas when you're tired. The others must have been thinking along the same lines.

I bring the subject up expecting to be placed in the position of defending a "no go" scenario. They unanimously decide we will take the third choice which is the long way around. It happens so quickly I'm not even sure it is my idea. Now I start to worry about the three factors I mentioned above—the surf at Malarrimo, the weather we will have to paddle into to get around Punta Eugenia, and the extra days it will add to the trip.

I think our decision is a relief to everyone. Glenn is relaxed in his folding chair reading a book. Jan is laying out on his space blanket reading. Dave is replacing the food we used in the plastic bottles with the vacuum packed food. He opens a package of rice or peanut butter and squeezes the contents into the plastic bottle we use it from. When the bottle is empty he refills it again. It works well and is an efficient system. I'm sitting on the beach working on my log and watching a sea lion ride the waves like a surfer. Two gulls are eating a small dead skate next to me on the beach. I wonder if they killed it or found it dead.

It's time to go to bed. In the morning the tide will be low and we will be able to see the rocks we have to negotiate to leave the beach. They don't seem like much of a problem because right now I have a full tummy, a mind without anxiety about a long crossing, and a good beach to sleep on. Life is good, and I wonder what the poor people are doing. Then I chuckle to myself as I realize we are the poor people.

DAY 7—MAY 22, 1992

We had such a good (and large) dinner that we slept very well. I wake up as it starts to get light—stretch—roll over, look at the ocean and sit up wide-eyed.

"Oh no!" I say out loud. I knew it was going to be bad, but not this bad. The tide is much lower than it had been when we landed the day before and the rocks stretch two hundred yards off shore with small two foot breakers rolling across them. The rocks are one to two feet in diameter, covered with green algae and barnacles. We can't carry the boats across because of poor footing. We can't drag the boats across because of the barnacles.

By now all of us are up and together we decide to carry the boats and gear a half mile down the beach where the band of rocks is only thirty yards wide. It takes many trips to carry the gear and the boats to our new launching place. By the time we move everything and repack the boats it is 9:20 a.m. and the tide is starting to come back in. Our launch is not bad because the water has come in enough so we can drag the boats a short distance without digging the bottoms out on the barnacles. The surf is only two feet and no problem. We would be in deep trouble if the surf were up. At 9:30 we clear the shore and start south. Our destination is Punta Baja. I am sure we can find a protected place to land on the south side of it.

We are seven and a half hours in transit before we round the point. To keep from being bored on the paddle we play a few word games, make up a few poems, share our expertise with each other and anything else to pass time. Glenn shares a cadence count with us.

> A yellow bird
> with a yellow bill
> sat upon
> my window sill.
> I lured it in,
> with crumbs of bread
> and then I smashed
> its yellow head.

Another favorite:

> Little Miss Muffet
> sat on her tuffet
> eating her curds and whey.
> Along came a spider
> and sat down beside her
> and said "Yo, bitch—what's in the bowl?"

There are many that I can't remember and others that I wish I couldn't remember.

Having no stakes for the tent, we used whatever was at hand on the beach. Over the course of the trip we used big rocks, bags of small rocks, sticks buried crosswise in the sand, old car tires, and whale bones.

We have been trolling our fishing lines as we paddle but no luck so far. We are all a little tired and sore. Each of us is sore in a different place but no one has escaped discomfort entirely. We have been out a week and tomorrow we'll take a rest day to let our bodies recover a bit. We are ahead of schedule and have no reason to push.

As we round Punta Baja the water smoothes out and is totally calm. We find a good beach at the mouth of a small canyon and land. There are a number of fishermen's huts here and twenty or so pongas. A ponga is an open boat about twenty feet long and is the common Mexican fishing boat. There is trash in the canyon that forms our little beach so we know we will have more rats than normal. There is no store or water available, but we don't need any supplies yet.

Glenn cooks up one of the culinary delights he must have learned from the master chef at some grammar school cafeteria. In the pot put four Top Ramen and one dehydrated beef stroganoff dinner for two. Bring to a boil and add corn flour tortilla mix until thickened to paste, or was it taste. It is great, but we are still hungry. Put more water in the pot—add instant mashed potatoes until thick—add powdered milk and Molly McButter to taste. We eat it all. Now we feel better. A cup of hot chocolate and it's bed time.

We put the food bags back in the boat and seal them in under the spray skirts so the rats can't get to them. Each of us digs out a little space on the beach to put a sleeping bag. We're glad we have our space blankets and waterproof bivy sacks because the nights are very damp and everything gets wet. I leave my paddling shirt out each night. When I get up in the morning it is soaking wet. I wring it out and put it on. This keeps the salt crystals from forming on the shirt and causing sores on my body.

Week Two

DAY 8—MAY 23, 1992

We don't hurry off the beach this morning. The sun is hidden behind the heavy overcast and it is hard to get motivated to climb back into the boats because we know it's going to be a short day. Our goal is Isla Geronimo, only ten miles away. The water is glassy smooth and there is no surf in our protected cove on the south side of Punta Baja.

I have been to Punta Baja on four different occasions, each time in a power boat that I was either taking south into Mexico or

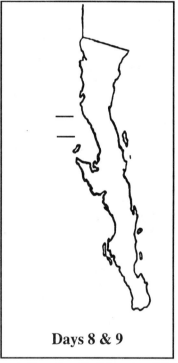

Days 8 & 9

bringing back north to Newport Beach, California. We anchored behind the point each time and every time there were twenty knot winds all night long. Now it is dead calm. I keep looking over my shoulder for those infamous big winds this place is known for.

At 8:00 a.m. we are island bound after an uneventful launch. We can see the island after about an hour of paddling and are enjoying the calm seas. Half way to the island we pass through a fleet of five pongas that have hooka divers on them.

The hooka divers are attached by an air line and safety line to the boat. The air compressor in the boat runs on a gas engine and pumps air to the diver through an umbilical line into a mask. These divers are using an older type of mask called a "Desco Mask" which is held tightly to the face by a web of straps. It is basically the same rig I used in the late nineteen fifties to dive commercial abalone off the Southern California coast. Their wetsuit's are one-half inch thick. I have never seen suits that thick. They are taking Green Abalone from about fifty feet of water. Processed abalone sells now in fish markets for about $85.00 a pound. Soon all the abs will be fished out here just like in California. Too bad!

We arrive at Isla Geronomo at 11:00 a.m. still under a heavy overcast. There are sand beaches all along the east side of the island, but they all have heavy sea lion populations on them. We don't want to disturb them so we choose a rock beach on the southern tip of the island. It is well protected from the north and if we are to get any bad weather it will most likely come from the north.

Glenn and Dave go diving as quickly as they can put their gear on. We can see how clear the water is and they are all turned on about it. Within minutes Dave has impaled a five pounder. As he wades into the beach he slips and falls and loses the fish off the end of his pole spear. He and Glenn look for it for fifteen minutes but never find it. They feel badly because they know it is going to die. They go back out and spear several more fish. They also bring in several "Red Rock Spiders." If you are not familiar with them, they look like lobster. You cook them in the same way you do lobster, and they taste just like lobster. We don't take any lobster, of course, because it is illegal for us to take them in Mexico.

Dave and Jan spend some time fixing one of the seats in their boat which has broken loose from the hull. One of our surf landings had done it in. It had to be fixed because of the support it gives to the hull. Our repair kit contains fiberglass cloth and resin and they soon have it repaired.

I take a walk up to the fishing village on the cliffs above us. No one is there except four of the ugliest chickens I have ever seen and a two hundred pound hog. I visit with them for awhile as I sit and look out at the ocean. There is a cross on the hill in memory of the fishermen that have perished in heavy seas. It is hard to imagine anyone dying in heavy seas now, as I look at a mirror finish on the still water as far as I can see.

I walk back to camp and Glenn has dinner ready. As we eat, we try to figure out what we might be able to do to help a small blind sea lion pup that has come up on our beach and is just lying there. We come to the conclusion that short of killing it quickly there is nothing we can do to help it. None of us can kill it. We use the excuse that we shouldn't interfere with nature, but we are just too soft hearted. Our excuse doesn't make any sense at all because what we are doing is just leaving it to starve to death slowly, but we feel vindicated because we are "letting nature take its course."

We like this island. We would all come back to spend a week anytime we had the chance. The only problem is that the normal weather conditions here are strong winds from the north. It would make a very hard ten mile paddle back to Punta Baja which is directly into the wind. If you weren't in a hurry and could take a few days to wait out the winds I think we all would highly recommend this place for a one week diving or fishing kayak trip.

Three fishermen round the point in their pongas and wave at us. They are coming home to the village after a long day of fishing. Glenn says he needs a little cooking oil so we can fry the next fish we catch. He finds a two ounce Pepto Bismo bottle on the beach, he washes it out and walks up the hill to the village. The fishermen give him some oil and we are ready for our next fish fry. All we need now is some fish.

DAY 9—MAY 24, 1992

We get up early and start to pack the gear this morning without any wasted time. Yesterday was a day of rest, today is a day to make miles. We are off the beach by 7:00 a.m. and wave good-bye to our little blind sea lion as we paddle between the rocks and into a light north wind. After an hour of paddling we decide to try the sail. There is some wind but not much. While Glenn and Dave hold the sails, Jan and I paddle. We are making about four knots. Then the wind dies and we all paddle for three hours. A wind comes up again that meets our new criteria for sailing. Glenn decides that we have to see two good white caps in different places at the same time before we have enough wind to make it worthwhile to put the sails up. The sails go up and the wind starts to increase. Within half an hour we are in a thirty knot wind and the boat is throwing up a rooster tail.

Glenn has his back arched as far back as he can lean towards me in the aft cockpit. The sail is pulling him clear out of the boat. He has his feet against the foot braces and his legs are locked against the hull trying to hold himself down in his seat. The seas are running eight feet now and we are surfing down steep faces at ten or twelve knots. The rudder system on the boat is not made for this kind of running and isn't enough to keep us at the right angle on the following seas, so I'm using my paddle as a secondary rudder. Using the two rudders I manage to hold us at a safe angle across the faces of the waves. They are big enough now that if we go straight down one of them at this speed we will dig in the nose and pitch pole end over end. I'm having a hard time keeping the paddle in the water to control the direction because I have to reach out and slap it flat on the water every fifteen or twenty seconds in a brace to keep us from rolling over. Rudder–brace–rudder–brace– rudder–brace. We are screaming and yelling and having a great time. Dave and Jan are off our starboard side a hundred yards surfing down the seas just like we are.

In the middle of all this fun we pass a place called Punta San Carlos. As we approach it we see a windsurfer. Then a dozen of them. Then a hundred of them. I have never seen so many windsurfers in one place in my life. In fact, I think there are more windsurfers in the water here than I have ever seen in my life all put together. I have no idea what the significance of the day—or the place is, but what a sight! They buzz us at twenty knots and we nod, but the wind and spray is so loud we can't hear each other when we yell. We can see their lips move but we can't hear them. We are all on maximum survival mode as we hang on and concentrate on the "second school of thought—Don't fall out of your boat."

Finally the wind gets so strong that a gust lifts Glenn up out of his seat and is about to launch him from the boat. It rips the sail out of his hands. The sail hits the water and the aluminum pole instantly breaks in half. Dave and Jan see we are in trouble and take down their sail. We put the sails away and paddle for another four hours. It is much safer paddling in these seas anyway, but not as much fun.

When we land we are five miles ahead of schedule and six miles north of Punta Canoas. Thanks to the wind we have made thirty-three nautical miles or thirty-seven statute (car) miles. A good day.

Standing on the beach I imagine I am in a huge sand blaster. The blowing sand is impossible to escape. We find a ring of rocks some other idiots who also made their way to this spot had piled up to try to create protection for themselves. The ring is two feet high and eight feet in diameter. We put our tent over the rocks and use them as a support to keep the tent from blowing down. It works well. We are all huddling in the tent, eating Top Ramen, and sharing how we had felt in the boats while we were sailing and hanging on by the skin of our teeth. We all had a great time.

Jan in a less than perfect lair. Often our sleeping accommodations were not the best.

The broken sail we fix by taking out the piece that broke on the right side and also by taking out the same piece on the left side. This makes the sail twenty-two inches shorter and reduces the sail area by about thirteen square feet. It will be easier for Glenn to handle in strong winds. The piece on the left we took out is the piece that had broken before and had been sleeved with the tent pole. The tent pole is back to normal now and we have a smaller but working sail again. Life is still good. We go to sleep.

DAY 10—MAY 25, 1992

We wake to a new day and a brisk wind that has been blowing all night. We want to get off the beach before the wind gets worse and makes the surf even more difficult, so we break our routine and don't fix breakfast. We get out by 6:50 a.m. and Glenn and I have no trouble getting through the surf. We manage to time it just right and miss the big waves. Dave and Jan get sucked out into a larger set of waves and have to put up with a scolding from Mother Nature but they come through right side up. Jan loses his second hat so I give him my back up canvas hat. With his short black stubble of a beard and the stark white wide brimmed hat, he makes quite a picture. When he smiles his white teeth are all you can see under the brim of the hat. The hat is much better than the cap he was wearing before because it protects his ears. They look like they are about to turn into ash and fall off from being exposed to the sun all day long.

We paddle for four hours and the wind changes direction just enough so we can sail. The wind is coming from our starboard side and with our type of rigging we can't sail into it. We hold our course as far to our right as we can but after three hours we have been blown in dangerously close to the crashing surf. We fold up the sails when the swells start to peak under us and paddle on, being careful to stay just behind the surf.

By now we realize skipping breakfast was really stupid. There are several additional comments made that imply the entire trip might even fall into that category. When you are hungry your whole attitude changes. We eat a granola bar and eight almonds each and that is all the food we have available on deck. What has happened to our great plan? Everything has been going so well that we have become complacent and forgot that the reason everything was going so well was that we had a good plan and were following it.

This is the first time we haven't followed the routine and we are paying for it now. We are starving. Worse than being hungry, we are losing stamina. We are running out of fuel for our 'engines.' We find we have to rest more often and longer than normal to give our bodies a chance to reach into that supply of ugly fat and use some of it for fuel. At 3:00 p.m. we round a small point and say, "this is it." We've covered our twenty-eight miles and are all tired and hungry.

As we work our way around the point, we see a ponga on shore. This is a good sign because the Mexicans know where the best place on the beach is to land. We cautiously proceed into the surf line. The waves are many, but not crashing, and we realize we are on a shallow sand shelf. We pass over the shelf and into the mouth of a beautiful lagoon. Warm calm water. A perfect campsite.

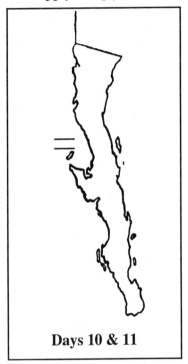

Days 10 & 11

The wind is still blowing and microsand is filling our ears, eyes and anything else it can find. We put up the tent and start making pancakes. We sit in the tent out of the wind and eat pancakes for an hour as fast as we can make them. We have no syrup or butter or anything to put on them but they are great. Finally we feel better. The others start doing the normal camp chores. Glenn is making small repairs on some equipment. Dave and Jan are moving the gear into a better position to protect it from the rats and are making sure the boats are high enough to be safe from the tide during the night. I continue making pancakes until I have enough for each of us to have three the next day for lunch. We aren't going to be hungry again. These pancakes are six inches in diameter and a half inch thick. With peanut butter on them they will give us the fuel we need for tomorrow's paddle. In two more days we should reach Santa Rosalillita (not to be confused with Santa Rosalia) which has a store. We will resupply there with more food and water.

We all take a walk back into the lagoon. We find tracks of our friends the coyote and the rabbit. This is an interesting lagoon. It is the mouth of a river that almost never has water in it. Because of the wet winter in Baja in 1992, the lagoon was cleaned out by the river water and was opened to the sea. Next year it will probably be sanded in and closed.

Glenn takes our small Pepto Bismo bottle up to a fisherman's hut and asks if he has any cooking oil. We used what we had cooking the pancakes. He does and Glenn fills our two ounce jar once again. Glenn asks if he can also spare a half pint of gas for our stove. Glenn's MRS stove will burn any fuel. The fisherman pulls out a can of Coleman fuel and gives us a half pint. He won't take any money so Glenn gives him a couple of the fruit bars that Dave had made before we left home. All of the fishermen we have met have done everything they could to help us in any way possible. The only thing they can't understand is why we are doing it. We tell them it is "just for sport." Then they seem to understand why we're doing it, and just think we're not too bright.

We cook up some Top Ramen and add a packet of freeze dried beef stroganoff for dinner. Dave can't eat beef because of a stomach problem so he has a packet of freeze dried chili beans. As the sun sets we have our hot chocolate and snuggle down into our sleeping bags to be lulled to sleep by Mother Nature's music, the sound of wind-blown sand hitting our bivy sacks.

DAY 11—MAY 26, 1992

A mouse runs across my face and I sit up in my sleeping bag. He jumps off my shoulder to the ground and is gone in the rocks. There is a glow in the East and it is time to get up anyway. No one else is stirring so I lay there for a few minutes and enjoy stretching and feeling the warmth of my bag. Why is it I always feel the most comfortable in my sleeping bag just when I'm supposed to get up? I think about how well our trip is going. We all seem to be getting stronger each day. We are averaging close to thirty miles a day and we are not whipped when we land any more. Jan generally goes running a few miles on the beach and Dave and Glenn explore the surrounding country side for hours.

We have sore spots in various places on our bodies but physically we are all fine. Our modus operandi has become a lifestyle. We have adapted well to it and the entire procedure of getting up, paddling nine hours, coming in through a surf line and setting up camp is just what we do. It isn't special any more. It is just like getting up and going to work every day.

Glenn is up now and the water is boiling. We eat, carry our gear to the water's edge, carry our boats down and pack the gear back into the compartments at either end. We all still have bags of various stuff between our legs in the cockpit too. We are lighter this morning because most of our water is gone. We will be in Santa Rosalillita tomorrow and can get more water there. There has been no need to make water for awhile. If necessary we can make more but that is one job we are doing our best to avoid. None of us enjoys pumping the reverse osmosis unit.

There is a south wind this morning. It is only five miles per hour but right in our faces as we paddle. If it builds just a few more miles per hour we will have a rough day. We are all quiet as we paddle. Could this be the storm the fishermen were talking about? The last couple of fishermen we talked to had mentioned a storm. After three hours the wind dies and our boats are gliding over mirror smooth water. I sense the relief in all of us. The sun is bright and warm. I notice that Glenn is slowing down his stroke rate. I slow down mine to match his. He slows down a little more. I match him again. I steer us up next to the other boat and I stop paddling. Glenn keeps going. I shout, "Wake up, Glenn!" He jumps and stops paddling. He has been asleep. I figure that has to be the height of conditioning when you can sleep and paddle at the same time. I'm sure I could master it except I have the extra duty of controlling the rudder and if I sleep we go in circles.

We are all impressed by the coast line—cove after cove of white sand beaches with small rocky headlands between them. There isn't a sign of a human for miles. After nine and a half hours we decide we've done enough for today and come in. We are at Punta Santa Maria. The cove we choose is seventy-five feet wide and is bordered by lava rock on both sides with white sand in between running back for one hundred feet. There is no surf and the water is clear. The sun is hot and there is no wind. It just doesn't get any better than this. Glenn lays out in the sand and takes a nap. I do, too. In my half sleep I go over the day's paddle.

We have seen more life in the ocean today than we have on the entire trip up to this point. Porpoise were all around us all day. We could see them jumping straight up fifteen feet out of the water all the way out to the horizon. Sea lions were numerous also. They would swim towards us until they could get a good look, generally about one hundred feet, then dive and leave. We could see them napping on the surface with their fins sticking straight up out of the water. Several times we got within thirty feet or so of them before they woke up. Then there would be a gigantic splash as they escaped the dragons that were almost upon them.

We also saw our first big shark. It was perhaps eight feet long and just under the surface fifteen feet to starboard as we passed. We scared it, too, I guess, because it dove in a hurry.

Just after we saw the shark I noticed our boat wasn't responding to the rudder. I called over to Dave and asked him if he could see why. He looked at our stern and said it is probably because the rudder has come loose and is being pulled along behind the boat by the cable. I had to agree with him—that would definitely cause a problem. We rafted the boats together and Jan took a six inch piece of nylon twine off his bow bag zipper and tied it through where the bolt has been holding the rudder on and we were back in business. We have spare bolts in our repair kit. Tonight, ashore we will fix it right.

Our lunch today was the pancakes I made the day before. We put peanut butter on them. A great lunch. The pancakes are made with pancake mix and one-third corn tortilla mix. They taste better and are more nutritious than just pancake mix. We tossed down six almonds for dessert. It's amazing but we considered this to be a really fine meal. I guess we have adapted to our new lifestyle.

I hear a noise and open my eyes. Dave and Glenn are putting on their diving gear. The ocean is clear and calm and they can't resist it. I know we are going to eat well tonight. Jan and I fix my rudder with a new bolt. This time we crimp the threads behind the nut so it won't work its way off. One of the major skills needed on an expedition like this one, I've decided, is the ability to be able to fix anything you bring with you. Everything breaks sooner or later.

I am very pleased with my Tofino boat. Having Necky build it of double layered Kevlar, both top and bottom, was a good choice. It functions well in both heavy sea and calm water. I never worry about it in the surf line and we punch into and through big surf with no fear of the boat failing. Our only limitations are our own skills. That's how it should be. Equipment should never be a limiting factor. If we don't complete the trip it should be because our skills failed, not our equipment.

Dave and Glenn still have leg cramps on occasion and Jan has hip pain because his seat is too narrow for his broad butt. I tell him if he didn't do squats in the weight room with hundreds of pounds on his shoulders he wouldn't have such a broad butt. He just gives me a smile that says, "Don't you wish you could do them?" He's right. The boils on my left leg are healed now but a rash under my right arm hurts when I paddle. I wash it every night and put Neosporin on it. It should be better in a few days. If I keep vaseline on it during the day it doesn't hurt much.

Jan and I take a walk along the coast and find a cove with turtle tracks on it. I am excited because turtles are not common any more. At least now we know there is one still around.

Our divers are back and we will have a pound or more of fried fish, Top Ramen, and two "Red Rock Spiders" each for dinner tonight—a perfect ending to a perfect day. We like this spot the best so far.

DAY 12—MAY 27, 1992

We ate so much last night it was hard to get up this morning, but nature called and got me out of bed. This is such a nice beach that we all would like to spend a few days here, but alas, we must move on.

Many of our camps were in gullies where we could lift our boats above high tide line. We didn't like these camps because they were always infested with rats.

We have the last of the John Slop for breakfast, pack the boats and push off through one foot breakers. It is 7:20 a.m.—a late start for us. The water is silky smooth. The porpoise jump all around us for hours. The sea lions are sleeping with their fins sticking high above the water again. They remind me of becalmed sail boats waiting for a wind. Our boats are so quiet we work at getting right next to them before they become aware of us. The reaction is always the same. Their heads slowly rise out of the water and they look at us with sleepy eyes. When it registers what we are and how close we are, we can almost hear them say, "Oh my God," and their eyes get as big as coffee cups. Instantly they explode in a burst of energy that sends them into a dive and throws a sheet of water ten feet into the air. They come up a hundred feet away and take a good look at us as we go on our way. I shout back to them, "Don't sleep on the main road to Cabo and you won't get run over."

We cover twenty-five miles in eight hours and come around the point into the bay where the town of Santa Rosalillita is. A couple of fishermen are anchoring their ponga off shore and we ask them where the store is. They point to a brightly colored building. We say, "Thank you," and go ashore.

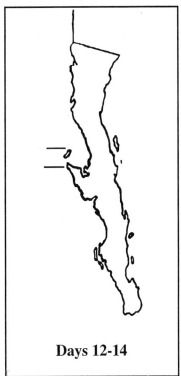

Days 12-14

The shore here is almost level and a small tidal difference exposes a wide sand beach. There are several cars driving along the beach. One drives up to us and the driver says, "Buenos dias." We ask him about water and he says, "follow me." We gather our water containers and follow him to his house which is an adobe building fifteen by twenty feet. Outside are three fifty gallon plastic water containers. With a pot he starts dipping water to fill our containers. Eleven gallons later everything we have is full. We carry them back to the boats. The tide is coming in so we move the boats up the beach a ways. Now it is time to hit the store.

When we leave the store our arms are full of oatmeal, oat bran, two *big* boxes of cookies, several cans of refried beans, oranges, and potatoes. After much asking we locate where the tortillas are made. We ask the lady for a kilo of tortillas and she tells us it will take forty-five minutes to make them. We say, "We'll be back in forty-five minutes." We wait at the boats and eat one of the big boxes of cookies. Several little kids are hanging around and share our cookies with us. The time is up and we go back to the store, buy more cookies to replace the ones we ate, and pick up the tortillas.

The wind comes up while we are ashore as it normally does in the afternoon and we decide to get back in the boats and sail for awhile. We don't like camping in towns. The wind holds steady and we cover eight more miles by 6:30 p.m. Folding our sails, we paddle around Punta Rosarito and turn into the wind to get ashore.

The shore here is a low headland just ten feet above the water. The wind blows across it most of the time and lays down the surf on the south side so the water is quiet right next to shore even if it is rough out a hundred yards. Because of this there is no surf to round off the rocks on the beach. The rocks are composed of lava and are very sharp. Bad for landing. We finally find a small patch of sand about twenty feet wide and land. We know the tide will be two feet lower when we leave in the morning so we check to see what is under the water. More sand. We are in good shape. We don't want to get caught again like we did at Rancho Socorro—with rocks we can't handle when the tide goes out. We are feeling good. We have plenty of water and supplies plus we are seven miles ahead of schedule.

For dinner we have rice which we mix with Velveeta Cheese. To this we add refried beans and tortillas. A big change for us. It is kind of like going out to dinner at a fancy place. We are being blessed with good weather and making the most of it. We made thirty-three miles today in ten and one-half hours of water time.

DAY 13—MAY 28, 1992

The weather is bright, clear and calm again this morning. The mice were a bit more of a nuisance than usual last night. Two of them crawled on me and I woke up both times. One went across my face, and the other was trying to share my sleeping bag with me.

The tide is just where we thought it would be and there is enough room between the rocks so we will have no trouble launching.

Seven a.m. seems to be the magical number. Every morning we push off the beach within ten minutes of seven. This morning it was 7:10. We decide to cut from point to point to save a couple of miles of paddling and set a course by compass for Morro Santo Domingo some twenty miles ahead. The sea is a slight chop from a seven or eight knot wind off our port bow. It is the kind of wind that is no problem except it is blowing off shore and is a little scary. If it picks up to twenty knots we could get caught six miles off shore in the middle of our crossing and have a hard time making it back in. We are all very aware of wind direction and speed as we paddle south.

The seals and porpoise keep us company like they have been doing for so many days now. At 1:00 p.m. we round the point and go ashore at the mouth of Laguna Manuela. We have lunch, look around the beach and rest a bit. When I was here before there were hot dog stands and many Mexicans from Guerrero Negro lounging on the beach. Now there isn't a soul. I don't know if it is the wrong season, the wrong day, or something happened I didn't know about. I have been telling the others all day long we would be able to get a hot dog here. (I don't know if they are disappointed or not, but whenever they walk by me the rest of the day they kick sand in my face.)

While we are on the beach the wind changes direction and picks up to twenty knots. We decide to sail for awhile.

Back in the boats, sails up, and we are again off. We sail well for about eight miles, but the angle of the wind has pushed us into a dangerous area right behind the surf. Glenn collapses the sail and puts it away.

Dave and Jan are farther out. They are using the sail my wife Sharon made and can sail off the wind better than we can. Glenn tucks the sail into the cockpit next to his seat and reaches for his paddle. One half of it is gone. In order to control the sail Glenn has used his paddle as a cross piece to spread the lines that support it. To put the sail up or take it down Glenn has to take the paddle apart in the middle. In the rough seas we are in, and with the big swells threatening to break on us, both Glenn and I have been preoccupied—Glenn with the sail and me with keeping the boat out of the breaker line. The left half of his paddle has slipped overboard.

We look back and can see it floating fifty yards back. I can't turn the boat around in the wind by myself so I back paddle for all I am worth and so does Glenn with the half paddle he has left. By keeping the rudder hard over, we are able to back up, retrieve the paddle and, luckily, stay out of the surf. We are so close that seven foot breakers are crashing just twenty feet past us. We get out of there in a hurry. "Once again we cheated death," I shout forward to Glenn. He waves his paddle in the air and then digs it in even harder as we knife our way out to sea to join Jan and Dave.

Another hour of paddling brings us to the mouth of Estero De San Jose. The bar here is a good mile wide and breaks for a half mile out to sea. As far as I can see there are breakers rising and crashing. The whole ocean is a breaker zone. "This should be interesting," someone said. We scrutinize it for about fifteen minutes from the edge of the zone. We talk about it and decide we can make it through. The tide is against us but not strongly and the wind is steady at our backs and will help. The tops of the breakers are being blown off so they are not crashing with the force they could be. Glenn and I choose a path into the shore at the corner of the lagoon and then turn our bow out and work our way around the shallow spots by paddling slightly out and along the beach, taking the smaller waves of the shore break in a broach and heading into the bigger ones. Dave and Jan elect to enter the bar farther up and take as little whitewater on the side as possible making for a straighter run. Either way we will be in both constant surf and very turbulent water for about half a mile. Instantly upon entering the surf line things get very exciting.

Glenn and I shoot straight into the small surf just off the beach and turn hard right. The waves are not very large—about two feet of whitewater—when they broadside us. We broach, Glenn digs his paddle in and the boat swings its stern around so we are headed out to sea again. We work our way a hundred yards around the shallow sand spit and turn down the main channel. Now the waves are three to four foot whitewater. We drop over one, broach, straighten out, broach again, and, "Wham!" the bungee cord that is tied to the fish line I am trolling is just about ripped off the boat. We have a big fish on the line. I should have pulled the line in before we entered the surf zone but forgot. Now we have a fish trying to pull us back out to sea.

Glenn says, "What is that noise?"

I tell him.

He says, "Cut it loose."

I say, "I can't." We leave it on and concentrate on the waves. It takes about twenty minutes to get through and into the bay side of the bar. We look over to see how Dave and Jan are faring and they seem to be okay about one hundred yards away. As we watch I think something is wrong. We can tell by the way their boat is acting in the two foot breakers that they are either fooling around or something isn't right. We paddle a course to intercept them and find halfway across the bar their rudder has broken. We had had to put up with a fish dragging behind us (that finally ripped off), but they had to cross the bar with no rudder control! As soon as we round the sand spit on the bay side, the water is dead calm and we haul out and fix their rudder. I never cease to be amazed at how Dave, Jan, and Glenn can fix anything. Sometimes I even help, but they rarely need my input.

We paddle on to the 'old wharf' in the lagoon. There is a dirt boat launch ramp here and we lift the boats to safety on the cliff. This is the old port where salt barges were loaded and taken to Cedros Island. When the bar filled in, creating the surf zone we just crossed, the station was abandoned. There is an old lighthouse and a dozen cement buildings here, all of which are trashed. Most are filled with broken glass and have been used as bathrooms by the locals for years. We are able to clean out one of the small rooms at the back of the complex and set up our stove out of the wind.

There seems to be two kinds of trash you can count on finding in Mexico no matter how far you think you are from civilization. One has been there for as many years as I have been traveling in Baja, which is about forty—the beer can. In the old days before aluminum cans it wasn't so bad. In a year or so they would rust away. Now they stay forever. The second item is worse. It has just appeared in the last ten years and seems to be everywhere—the disposable diaper. From where I am sitting I can see four diapers laying in the dirt. Besides the health hazard which is obvious, the aesthetic factor is worse. They don't ever degrade. They just lie there and smell. This is a recreation area for the local town of Guerrero Negro. It is too bad the people don't understand the pollution problem.

We eat our Top Ramen with dehydrated mixed vegetables in it and discuss tomorrow over our chocolate before going to sleep. The next few days could be hard ones. We have to cross another bar going out the mouth of

Scammons Lagoon, land on Malarrimo Beach which is famous for its big surf, and then paddle about forty miles into the prevailing wind and seas to get around Punta Eugenia. We can't plan anything because there are so many variables. We'll just do what we've been doing—figuring it out when it happens.

Jan and Glenn sleep by our cooking gear back in the complex. Dave and I sleep next to our boats out on the cliff. The wind is brisk and cool. It feels good.

DAY 14—MAY 29, 1992

The wind blew all night, but only eight or so knots, and there is a lot of moisture in the air. Things are always wet in the morning but this morning everything is really soaked. I have to wring out my shirt and pants before I put them on. One good thing about getting out of a warm sleeping bag and putting on wet clothes in a brisk wind is I wake up in a hurry. It gives me great motivation to get the boats packed and start paddling so I can get sealed up out of the wind under my spray skirt. I put my nylon windbreaker on over the top and I'm pretty much wind-chill proof.

On several occasions we have put our life jackets on to try to stay warm. When the wind velocity is high and the seas dump on you every few minutes so you are totally soaked for hours at a time, nothing seems to help except paddling harder. As long as we continue to eat well we can produce enough heat through paddling to keep us going. Today rough water isn't going to be a problem.

We are inside the lagoon. Even with high winds the water is calm. There is heavy overcast and the soft gray light makes the swamp lands ahead appear impenetrable. We know there is a channel through to the other side and into Scammons Lagoon. As we move along the barrier island that forms the lagoon, we watch the sand blow off the tops of the dunes and build up on the downwind side. If I could watch in time lapse, I could see the dunes walk across the island. I don't have a hundred years to sit and watch, so I just imagine it.

After eight or so miles the channel through the swamp narrows and divides, and we have to start choosing which channel we will take. I make several choices and we finally find ourselves in a small channel six feet wide with a dead end up in front of us. The tide is going out rapidly and we are about to get stranded. Jan looks around and shakes his head and says, "I hate this. I hate the swamp. I hate the mud and I hate the overcast. Let's get the hell out of here and get back in the open ocean." We all agree, but the problem right now is how.

Glenn and Dave get out of the boats and walk in different directions to scout out where we are. They come back and say there is a clear channel three hundred yards to our right. To paddle back and around is four or five miles. We decide to drag the boats across the swamp mud instead.

We rig four lines about twenty feet long to the bow of one of the boats. Each of us takes a wrap around the waist and over the shoulder and we start to pull. The boat slowly breaks loose from the mud and starts to move. It weighs about four hundred pounds with all our gear and water. Once we get it moving we start to run. Our feet are sinking into the mud up to our knees. Several times I fall but get up and catch the others and keep pulling until we are at the water's edge in the new channel. This is the most tiring thing we have done on the entire trip. I am gasping for air. We go back and do the same thing to the second boat, except we don't run. We just walk fast to keep it moving and it is much easier on this old man.

Once again we are going along in calm water. We emerge out of the channel into a huge bay and see tug boats pulling the big salt barges. One is on its way out full of salt, and one is on its way back from Cedros Island, empty. At

Cedros the barges are unloaded and create a pile of salt that is bigger than two football fields and fifty feet high. When they get enough to fill a ship, a big freighter comes into the tie-down buoys to be filled via a long conveyer belt. The reason salt is barged to Cedros is that there is deep water right next to shore so the big ships can come in and tie up.

We don't want to get in their way so we find a small piece of sand that becomes exposed as the tide goes out and forms a fifty by one hundred foot island right out in the middle of the bay. We pull up on it and have lunch as we watch the tugs manipulate the barges through the channel. The tug is tied to the side of the barge as it leaves the dock and moves through the narrow channel inside the bay. Near the mouth of the bay the tug stops, cuts loose, and moves up front with a long tow cable for the open ocean crossing.

Glenn pulls the boat across a shallow spot in the middle of Scammon's Lagoon.

We finish our peanut butter, tortillas, and granola bars and try to catch the barge that is going out to sea. Jan and Dave finally catch it and get sucked into the eddy behind it. They pull up within several feet of the barge and could stay with it due to the water sucking them along right off the transom. Glenn and I don't get that close and never get into the suction. The barge is making six knots and we can't stay with it for more than ten minutes or so. Dave and Jan drop off and wait for us. We catch them right at the mouth of the lagoon.

The mouth of Scammons Lagoon is about two miles wide. If we go north and west we can paddle out several miles and then turn back south and avoid the bar and the breakers, but this would be an extra five or six miles which means two hours of paddling. We decide to cut to the west shore and work our way through the breakers, across the bar, and on down Malarrimo Beach. There are breakers as far as we can see from shore to about two miles out to sea. The swells are big, perhaps ten or twelve feet, but they aren't breaking hard. They are spilling off the top and the whitewater is rolling gently down the face about three feet high. We tell ourselves we can handle this stuff. No problem. All we have to do is be careful and not get caught with the boat in a bad attitude.

It becomes a rather exciting couple of hours. There are moments when we question our judgement. I guarantee none of us got bored during the paddle, but we have no problems and find ourselves through the bar and on our way. Whenever we find ourselves having met a challenge like crossing this bar we spend an hour or so telling each other how great we are. Strangely enough, if we screw up we never mention it. This phenomena is called "selective memory."

The water is very sloppy. The wind is at twenty knots on our right beam which means the water is washing over us constantly. We note with pleasure the water is warm, much warmer than it has been. The sun is out and we are loving it. Jan is feeling good now. No more mud and we aren't lost in a swamp. I paddle best if it is overcast and cool but Jan is truly solar powered. He likes it hot.

Jan says, "My butt hurts." All of us hurt somewhere on our body and it's 3:30 p.m. anyway, so we decide to go in. There is a long surf line extending out from shore as far as we can see down the beach so it doesn't really matter where we do it. Glenn and I point the bow to shore, tie everything on deck a little tighter and go for it. This has been one of our major concerns, the surf on Malarrimo Beach.

We time the swells and take off behind a big one. We're doing just great until the next one catches us. We back paddle but not quite hard enough. The front end drops over the edge just as the wave breaks. For an instant as the nose drops down I am held three feet in the air above the wave and I watch Glenn disappear under the foam. Microseconds later I am sucked down and join him. The boat drops about six feet and hits hard. I am completely underwater and am leaning as far as I can to my right into the wave. My paddle is thrust out its full length as I stick it into the base of the wave. I know Glenn, four feet in front of me, is doing the same thing. I can tell we are still upright because I can feel the hull of the boat slamming along the water as it is being rushed towards the beach. After what seems like minutes but was probably twenty or twenty-five seconds our heads pop out and we can breathe.

We ride the broach another sixty or seventy feet until the wave dissipates to three feet. I push my paddle down hard to stop my end of the boat from sliding and at last we swing around and the wave passes us. We hustle like crazy before the next one catches us, but it does anyway and we broach one more time on a smaller wave and reach shore safely. Glenn is out of his cockpit and has the boat pinned to the beach so quickly there is no way we can wash back out.

We look back to see how Jan and Dave are doing and they are on the inside break and are in good shape. We're all full of excitement again and spend the next hour, as we unload the boats and move them up the beach, expounding to each other one more time just how wonderful we are. Our surf skills are definitely much better than when we started, and we are learning what the boats can and can't do.

We are starting to feel "at home" in our cockpits. It's a feeling that's hard to explain. I have never spent enough time in a kayak to really feel "at home" in it. After fourteen days, my subconscious is recognizing it as my home, and it will remain my home for at least another twenty days. It feels good. All of us have a sense of security when we are in our boats and out to sea. It seems that to chase a dream makes the chaser a slave to the dream. The four of us are each slaves unto our own dream. Only a slave would be found living under the conditions we live in, and feeling more at home and secure out at sea in a kayak than on land is almost demented. Luckily we have benevolent masters.

We get organized and look around the beach and are fascinated. I have a complete whale skeleton lying here right in front of me. There is also a huge cedar tree four feet in diameter and sixty feet long laying on the beach. It has to have come from the Pacific Northwest, a journey of two thousand miles. We also, of course, find trash that was dumped from a Princess Cruise ship—their name is written all over it—but at least no disposable diapers. It is a great place. All the books expound on how good this beach is for beachcombing. They are right.

The wind is 'honking on' so we put up our tent to get out of the blowing sand. We hold the tent down with whale bones and use the vertebra as chairs. I go into the water and wash off with some Selsun Blue shampoo I found on the beach that has Princess Cruise Lines written on the side. We made about twenty-eight miles today and are still a few miles ahead of our schedule.

We eat dinner (Top Ramen, of course) and chat about our next forty miles. We will have the wind and chop on our right side all the way. It seems two twenty mile days will be just about right—long enough to get us around Punta Eugenia, and short enough that beating into the weather will not be too bad. We indulge ourselves with hot chocolate and dig into the sand for a good night's sleep.

I dream of whales all night long. It is the first time I have ever slept totally surrounded by whale bones.

Week Three

DAY 15—MAY 30, 1992

I slowly become aware that I am waking up. The warm sleeping bag is comfy cozy. I stretch and start to snuggle in for another hour or so, but then I remember where I am, on the beach in Baja. I pull back the edge of my bivy sack and peek out. I can't see a thing. I am in the tent. I listen for the wind. It's still there, but not as strong as it was. My moving around awakens Glenn and, like magic, the breakfast water is on the stove.

The surf is not real big yet and we hustle a bit faster than usual to get off the beach. We want to get

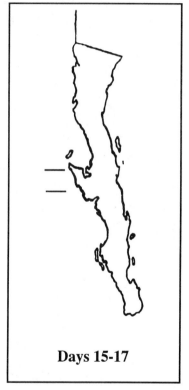

Days 15-17

in as much mileage as we can before the wind picks up. By 6:30 a.m. we are eating breakfast and breaking camp. Our boats are at the water's edge and packed. We are dressed in our wet paddling gear and sealing ourselves into our boats.

The beach is shallow, creating a long wave line with five whitewater faces rolling in at a time, but they are not super big—about five feet. Glenn and I are first off the beach with a push from Jan and Dave. We punch through the first wave and move on to the next. This one is bigger and washes our faces. The next two are big enough that we both disappear under them as they roll over us.

There is a big sucker outside and coming fast. We paddle as hard as we can and try to get over it before it breaks. It looks like we're going to make it—no, I don't think we are—maybe—no—paddle harder. As the wave reaches to the skies seven feet above us the bow of our boat shoots up the face. The wave breaks. Glenn is through it but I catch it right in the face. The momentum of the boat carries us up the face and in a few seconds I break clear and find our boat flying through the air. The boat, being rather poorly designed for flying (no wings), drops out of the sky and falls five or so feet to slam back into the water. I let out a cheer that joins with Glenn's "All right!"

We keep paddling for another fifty yards to clear the surf zone and then turn to watch Dave and Jan come out. It is like watching an instant replay of our exit. When they reach us behind the surf they are well washed and have piloted their boat for a few seconds through the air like we had. We rudder our boats to the west and the work day begins.

The weather holds and the wind stays at around twelve knots. No problems. After seven hours we reach a point where we can land. There is a sand beach and only three foot waves. We look ahead to the next point about three miles or so away and I say, "It's still early. We can get over there in less than an hour and be much closer to Punto Eugenia if the weather kicks up tomorrow." They agree and we head for the far point.

The wind takes a sudden shift and instead of coming off our starboard bow it is coming right in our faces. It slows us down a bit. After another thirty minutes it shifts again and is coming directly off the land where we want to go. We are still a mile out when the full impact of the wind catches us. It increases to thirty knots and just howls around us. We have our heads down and are paddling too hard to talk. Slowly we inch our way to shore. The last mile takes forty-five minutes of all out effort. The others decide the only good thing about my decision to cross to this point is if we die it isn't their fault.

We land a quarter of a mile inside the point on a rock beach in front of a small ravine. There are several fairly nice houses on the point and a lighthouse. A Mexican comes up in his new pickup, gets out and visits for awhile. His name is Eddie. He lives on the point and has been there for several years. He fishes. Everybody that lives out here fishes. There isn't anything else to do. We carry the boats up into the ravine to get them above high tide line and pitch our tent on top of the bluff. The wind is still intense. We use big rocks to hold the tent down.

We have calm, protected water off the beach in front of us so Dave and Glenn go diving. Dave comes back with an eight pound "rock spider." It is the biggest one I have seen for a long time. The total catch at the end of the dive is five fish and seven "rock spiders." We fry the fish, boil the rock spiders and then use the same water to cook our Top Ramen to give it a 'rock spider' flavor. It is a great meal.

We have been on what is known as the "destruction coast" for two days now and only have one more day, about twelve miles, to go. The weather here is usually much rougher than we have encountered. I think the little guardian angel pin a cousin gave me to wear on my hat the day we started the trip is doing her job well.

If the weather holds tomorrow we will make it around Punta Eugenia and will all breathe easier.

We have our hot chocolate, climb into our sleeping bags on the hard, rocky ground, cross our fingers hoping the wind will die down over night, and go to sleep.

DAY 16—MAY 31, 1992

When I wake up I listen for the wind. Everything is still. There is a deep red glow and I am confused for a second. I realize I am in the tent and the sun coming through the red canvas makes a red world for me to wake up to. My mind is not quite awake yet and I fantasize I am in a scene from the Bradbury story, "The Martian Chronicles," but I don't think they had oatmeal for breakfast.

We are all up now and our camp is doing its morning disappearing act. I am amazed every morning as the huge pile of bags, boxes and miscellaneous 'stuff' find its way through the hatches and out of sight. Our packing is totally automatic now. Everything has its exact spot in the boat and there is an exact order for each piece to be stowed.

As we eat our breakfast we all wish we still had some John Slop left. What we are eating now is Mexican oatmeal. It is really bland. We add salt, sugar, powdered milk and some Molly McButter powder. It's edible but just barely. We eat a lot of it. Jan even pretends he likes it.

We leave the beach at 6:45 a.m. and our prayers have been answered. The sea is calm. After an hour a six knot wind comes up in our face and I get a little worried that if it builds we might have a hard time getting around Punta Eugenia. This has been one of my major anxiety points since early in the planning stage. I have come around Punta Eugenia on several previous occasions, in big boats, and have had a hard time of it. I know how rough it can get.

Two hours later we paddle around the point in flat, glassy water. Not even a ripple. There is a village on the west side of the point and we think about going in for awhile but decide to paddle on and take advantage of the flat water to make some miles.

At noon we raft the boats together to have some lunch. Glenn opens his spray skirt, holds his nose and says, "This is a good place for a stick up." We all know what he means. The air in the sealed cockpit can get pretty rank with all the wet gear, sweat, and various outgassing from the paddler. We drop the subject and eat lunch. We don't have much—some fruit bars, a few almonds, and a small piece of jerky.

Pancakes were quick and easy if we were starving when we reached shore. Glenn cooks while Dave rests.

We paddle until 2:00 p.m. and decide that's enough for today. We have made one hundred twenty miles in four days. We are around the point and the town of Tortuga is farther than we want to paddle today. We don't like camping near towns anyway. We come in around Punta Rompiente and land through some small three foot surf.

We are hungry so we make pancakes again and stuff ourselves. We take a health inventory and decide we are all okay. Lots of little festering sores, like hang nails, small cuts or scrapes are on our feet and hands, and Jan's callus on his foot is tearing off but there's nothing we can't live with.

Tomorrow we will take a short paddle into Bahia Tortugas and resupply. We should have access to a radio phone and I can call home and tell Sharon, who will inform everyone else, that we are doing well and are on schedule.

DAY 17—JUNE 1, 1992

There is a slight offshore breeze when I wake in the morning. Glenn is out of his bag and lighting the stove before I can get my second eye open. Dave and Jan are up, too, and getting gear organized. We are all anxious to get to Tortugas and find the store. We launch easily, getting our faces washed in a couple of waves but not getting pounded at all. The sea is ripply but smooth and the porpoise keep us company all the way into Bahia Tortugas.

We step out of the boat at 10:30 a.m. and some men come down and help up lift the boats to dry ground. Because of all the help we don't have to unload them to make them light. One of the men says he will show us where the bakery, store, and phone are. We say thank you and we're off.

The bakery is first and we buy three bags full. By the time we walk four blocks to the phone building one bag is already empty. I go in to make a call and the others go on to get supplies at the store.

Making a call from one of these isolated towns is an interesting procedure. There is one phone in town. It is a radio phone so when you talk on it the sound fades in and out. I go in and sign my name on the waiting list. I am number nine. When a person is through the girl at the desk dials the number for the next person on the list. When the connection is made they call you and you pick up the phone in a phone booth in back of the counter. It takes an hour but I get through. I tell Sharon we are okay and still on schedule. I pay the lady twelve dollars and fifty cents and go looking for the others. I find them with arms full of food from the store and both of the remaining bakery bags empty.

Our most difficult landing and campsite was on this "Beach from Hell." Landing here was the worst decision made on the trip. Unfortunately I made it. I still can't believe that no one was hurt.

We carry the food back to the boats. With great skill we manage to get all the new 'stuff' stuffed. Now it is time to go for fresh water. We find a park two blocks from the beach that has a hose on a tap. I carry my two-quart deck bottles, a two-gallon plastic jug, and a two-gallon mylar bag that had started the trip filled with John slop. The others are all carrying about the same. We fill everything with water and take it back to the beach. Now we have to carry the boats down to the water, about one hundred feet, and there are no other people around to help. We manage, but just barely. We stow the water in the boats and shove off at noon. We have full tummies and lots of water. We are all smiles. Our plan is to cross the bay and get away from town before we camp. It is going to be a semi-rest day.

When we get across the bay it is only 1:00 p.m. and the seas are still calm. We decide to go around the point and pick up a few more miles. By two o'clock the wind has come up from the north and water is whitecapping so we sail down the coast. By three o'clock the wind reaches twenty-five knots and we are really moving.

We drop sails as we round Morro Hermoso and paddle hard to stay close to shore to look for a place to land. There is a large south swell crashing on the beaches. As far as I can see there are steep cliffs one hundred fifty feet high with waves crashing against them. Perhaps, I think to myself, we may have to spend the night out. The wind is howling at twenty-five knots from the north, and the seas are running five feet. The swell is running eight feet and is from the south. We would have no problem in daylight, but I am concerned about being out in this condition in pitch blackness. I am really looking hard for any place we might sneak in. Finally, I see a steep canyon cutting its way through the cliff. There is a rock beach and room to pull the boats high enough to be above the high spring tide that will occur tonight. From our position a quarter mile away it looks great. We head for it. Looking ahead along the cliffs there is nothing else even possible.

In close to the cliff the wind is no problem—only the south swell will test us. As we close on the beach we see the rocks that look six inches in diameter from out at sea are really two feet in diameter. The beach is at a forty-five degree angle, which is as steep as it can get, and the surf is a shore break with eight-footers crashing on the rocks at all times. We go in close to get a good look. Just about the time I decide to "just say no" and move on we are picked up by a wave and have little choice but to go for it. We shoot up the steep beach perfectly, right behind the foaming front of the breaker. We hit the rocks with a jolt and before we can do anything the water disappears through the space between the rocks and we are sliding backwards, along with some fifty pound boulders rolling down the beach beside us to meet the next crashing breaker.

By now we both know we've been had. We both are back paddling for all we're worth to try to punch through the next wave before it breaks. "Oh shit!" We probably said it in unison. The stern lifts as the next shore pounder forms. We give it everything we have in reverse. We're not going to make it. I look down as the bow drops at a forty five degree angle and all I can see in front of the boat is big boulders, and no water. What seems to be a long time passes from the time I look directly at the boulders until I feel the boat accelerate forward. "This is it. We've had it. There is no way the boat can survive." I temporarily believe the trip has come to an end.

We shoot into the rocks, careen off one rock that is bigger than the others, and bounce up the beach. Glenn tosses his paddle up onto the beach and is out of his cockpit before our forward motion stops. I dig my paddle into the rocks and hold as tight as I can. I'm afraid the paddle is going to break but it doesn't. Glenn grabs the bow and digs in. The boat drags us down the beach about six feet. The next wave crashes on the stern, and the boat and Glenn shoot up the beach again. All I can think about is Glenn getting caught under the boat, but he throws his body across the bow of the boat and gets his legs up in the air as we shoot up the beach again. This time with Glenn hanging on and me digging in with the paddle, we stick. I jump out with more speed than I have ever mustered before or since and we are ready to move the boat up high on the next wave. Two more tugs and we are above high water mark. I look at Glenn and say, "We're alive."

He replies, "I can't believe it!"

Dave and Jan are on their way in. They time it just right, like us on our first wave, and shoot up the beach. We are there to grab their bow. The beach is so steep that Jan jumps out in knee deep water and Dave jumps out in water over his head. The next wave washes all of us in a tumble up the beach.

When we are all above high water we sit down to recuperate. We are so stoked we are talking all at once. No one is hurt badly, only a few bruises. It is only then the others remember who chose this landing. I can't remember just what they said about it, but it wasn't very complimentary to my eyesight, judgement, or lineage. Jan does say he was sure Glenn and I were "goners" and couldn't believe we pulled it off. That makes me feel better. At least my "true grit" level isn't too bad even if my judgement is.

We find ourselves making camp on a steep face among large boulders. I move a lot of rocks to make a fairly level platform to sleep on. The others make similar adjustments to the mountain to try to have a good night's sleep. We all are very aware that in the morning we are going to have to leave this "Mother of All Beaches." None of us has figured out just how we are going to manage that little chore yet. We will tend to that problem in the morning. Who knows, maybe it will be dead calm.

We have hot chocolate and cookies to celebrate being alive with no broken bones and crawl into our sleeping gear.

DAY 18—JUNE 2, 1992

I wake up and peek out of my bivy sack. It is pitch black. I get up, and go to the bathroom. I get back in my bag, but I can't get back to sleep. The waves are crashing thirty feet below me on the rocks and I can't get over the thought that we are going to have to get through them in just a few hours. I count the crashes. They are only ten to twelve seconds apart, too close together to push off the beach and get through. There is about a twenty second break every ten or twelve waves. I think we will just have to time it right. Nothing could be worse than to not make it over the incoming wave and be smashed backwards onto this beach from hell. Finally I get back to sleep.

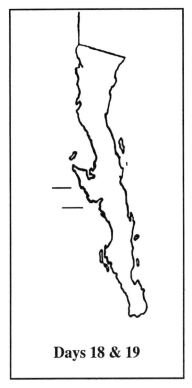

Days 18 & 19

We get up in the morning with mixed feelings. I can tell all of us would just like to stay in our sleeping bags and not face this beach, but we are soon up and moving the gear down the beach as usual. We all know the longer we wait the worse it can get.

Dave is complaining about a rat that bit him during the night. There is a hole in his finger. I had a mouse crawl across my face and wake me up but he didn't bite me. We don't think much about the mice and rats anymore. They crawl on and around us every night. Dave asks, "Do they carry any disease?"

I tell him, "I'll know the answer to that question in about a week."

He says, "Thanks a lot."

We all put our heads together and try to figure out the best way to get off the beach. We decide to go with Glenn's plan of the PAP launch. PAP stands for "Push and Plunge." We think it will work. We load the boats and ready them just above the high water line. I get in the aft cockpit of my boat and seal up. They seal up the front cockpit so no water will come in. I take the paddle and put my hands in the right position to paddle, then I lean forward and extend my left arm forward and bring my right hand in against my side so the paddle is lying along the top of the boat. This gets the paddle out of the way, and when the time comes to paddle I will be instantly ready. Dave gets on one side of the boat, Jan on the other, and Glenn on the stern. We count and watch, waiting for the right moment. Glenn seems to be best at reading the swells so the call is up to him.

A wave crashes and races up the beach. "NOW!" screams Glenn, and I am catapulted into the water. I am a twenty foot long projectile propelled by a paddle that is moving so fast it is just a blur. Fear is the world's best motivator. A wall of water is forming in front of me.

My mind flashes back to the martial arts story I used to tell my students in self defense classes. *A boy and an old man are sitting on the hillside when a rabbit comes running down the path. Right behind the rabbit is a fox. The boy says, "The rabbit is dead. The fox can run faster." The old man says, "Not necessarily so. The fox is just running for his dinner. The rabbit is running for his life."*

The wave face rises before me as I punch through and over the top. For a few seconds I hang in the air and then drop into the calm water beyond the danger zone. The rabbit has escaped. I turn to watch Jan get launched the same way I had. I can see the determination in his eyes as he beats the water on his way out. He disappears behind a wall of water and then breaks through to join me in the calm water beyond the surf.

We have accomplished the "Push" part of the PAP launch, Now Glenn and Dave take the "Plunge" and swim out to the boats. They climb into their respective cockpits and we are all excited again because we made it. We decide if we ever fail in a PAP launch we will refer to it as a "PAP smear," because it would be uncomfortable and very embarrassing.

Our nine hour paddle is mostly done on flat water. The big Pacific swells that roll under us are of no concern out here in open ocean. At sea we can handle almost any condition without trouble. The problems occur when we cross the land-sea interface, commonly called the surf zone.

We round Punto San Pablo at 4:30 p.m. and see a calm cove to land in. There is a fisherman's house on the hill and we land in the ravine next to it.

The fishermen come down and invite us up to get water. Dave and Glenn go diving, and Jan and I go up to the house.

The house is much better than most we have seen. It is constructed of plywood instead of branches. It has a porch and two rooms. There are two pads on the floor in one room and two old wood chairs. The shocking thing is to see an old television set in the corner. I ask where it came from. Our host says, "un momento," and goes out to a shed in back. He pours some gas into a small engine and starts a Honda generator. The TV set comes on. He tells me to watch it while he goes out and starts moving a TV dish around by hand until I tell him to stop. We watch the six o'clock news from somewhere in California. The two fishermen don't speak any English and they can't get any Mexican stations, so they say they don't watch it much.

They bring out several live abalone. They shuck them out of the shell, cut them horizontally and vertically so they are diced in quarter inch squares. We put lime juice, garlic powder, and hot sauce on them and eat them raw. Glenn and Dave join us and together we each eat a whole abalone. Jan whispers in my ear, "I can't believe I'm eating this raw shit, but it's great."

We fill our water bottles from a hose that is gravity fed from a tank in back. The water is brought in by truck. The end of the hose is hanging on a hook from the roof of the porch. To get water we just lower the end of the hose. At about three feet from the ground water comes out. We fill our deck bottles and hook the hose back to the roof.

We thank our new friends and go down to our camp where we have dinner of Top Ramen with fish cut up in it. We dine in an old broken ponga that is pulled up on the beach. It is great. We are protected from wind and blowing dirt. We go to bed knowing that when we wake up tomorrow, yesterday will have been an especially good day.

DAY 19—JUNE 3, 1992

I wake up with a start. It is still dark but I can see the suggestion of a glow in the sky to the east. I lie wondering what woke me up. Suddenly I feel something moving around in my sleeping bag. I fight the urge to jump up and get out of it. I know there are a lot of rattlesnakes here. If it is a rattler and I squeeze it, I'll have a bad problem. I lie perfectly still for three or four minutes that seem much longer than that. I feel it again moving slowly over my stomach. It is small, light, and I can feel the feet walking on my skin. I know it's not a snake, just another mouse.

I unzip the sleeping bag slowly. When the zipper opens to my stomach, the little bugger leaps out and runs up my chest over my face, and, before I can move, it's gone. Then I laugh because I realize he was lost in there and must have been terrified. Can you imagine being lost in a pitch black catacomb and hearing the sound of a zipper approaching you? What great stories he'll have to tell his grandchildren.

I decide to get up. The wind is five miles an hour off shore. This is a good sign because it will keep the sea calm and should shift to an on-shore wind around noon when the land warms up.

Everyone is up now and doing the morning routine. We all move around the beach with specific chores that no longer take any thought. All the preparation to launch through the surf just seems to happen now. It's almost like someone else is doing it. We're uneventfully through the surf line at 6:45 a.m. and start our paddle for Bahia Asuncion thirteen miles down coast. We play word games and movie quizzes to pass the time and by 11 a.m. we round the rocky point and come to rest on the beach at Bahia Asuncion.

There are kids on the beach and a few people around so I stay with the boats while the others go looking for a store. A tall slender gringo comes down the beach and asks, "Who are you guys?" He appears to be in his fifties. It is hard to tell because of his full beard and his weathered skin. He looks a bit like a rusty washboard with mold on it. I tell him who we are and where we came from.

"I saw you dudes making it around the point," he says. You really make those things move."

I tell him, "We do the best we can."

"All the way from San Diego. Damn, that's far out."

I ask his name.

He writes it in the sand. "B E A L—Tom Beal" he says.

I ask where he is from.

"All over. Hell, I've been everywhere. For the last five months I've lived right here. I was surfing down here and my car broke down and these great people just took me in. They got great big hearts. Hell, I don't have no money but I eat good, drink beer, and got a place to sleep. What more could a man ask for? These are great people. They got big hearts. They just took me right in. Everybody down here knows me. I drove up the coast about thirty miles to a little fishing village and when I told them my name they knew all about me. These are great people."

Later we would talk about old 'TB' amongst the four of us. We feel sorry for the poor Mexicans that helped the gringo whose car broke down and then couldn't get rid of him. When he said proudly that, "they know all about me up and down the coast," we felt that was a true statement, but he wouldn't have said it so proudly if he realized he was probably referred to as a free loader.

He was a typical "flower child" out of the 60's. As we left the beach he blessed us and said he could feel we were going to be all right the rest of the way. He also told us he was "well connected with the spirit world," and he would "put in a good word for us." We all really felt better now that Tom Beal was on our side.

Whenever we would beach near a fishing village the locals would come talk to us. This youngster is fascinated by Dave's funny looking "ponga."

The wind is picking up. Glenn takes out our sail and away we go. Dave and Jan are sailing off to our right. Jan and I keep paddling in our respective boats to aid the sail and pick up a little speed. After two hours the wind is up to twenty knots and we are making good time on sail alone. A little after 5:00 p.m. we put ashore behind Punto San Hipalita. We have covered thirty-three miles. A good day and we are right back on schedule.

When we round the point, we have to paddle back into the wind to make the beach. By the time we swing out to clear the rocks and reefs projecting off the point, we have about a mile to paddle back into the cove to land. The wind is sweeping down off the cliffs with a real vengeance. We are paddling with all the strength we have and just making perhaps one mile an hour. Jan shouts across the wind blown white caps, "Where are you now, Tom Beal, when we need you?"

Glenn shouts back, "Just remember what school of thought you belong to." We all laugh and then dig in again. The slightest rest and we lose ground.

There is a small village ahead of us on the mesa above the beach. Two people are sitting in front of a low building out of the wind watching us. Ten minutes pass, we are a little closer to shore. I look up and there are twenty people standing there watching us. Ten more minutes pass, we are getting closer now and the crowd has grown to fifty people. We finally enter the surf and ride it into the beach about a quarter of a mile from the village. All of the people come running down the beach to watch us land. There are kids everywhere. Cars full of women. Old men on crutches.

Glenn looks at me and says, "I don't think they see many outsiders here." They help us carry our gear and boats up the beach and then they all go back to their homes in the village—all that is, except the kids. They stay and help us put up the tent and then five of them crowd into it with us. We give them an almond and a hard candy. They don't know what the almond is. They taste it and two of them spit it out. The other three are either brave or polite and swallow it. They like the candy.

We make our Top Ramen for dinner, drink our hot chocolate and turn in. It's been a long day, but we rest well tonight knowing the "well connected" Tom Beal has said a "good word for us."

DAY 20—JUNE 4, 1992

There is a deep red glow in the sky as I get up and feel the breeze on my face. It tells me the wind has been blowing inland all night. As we dismantle camp, we wonder where all the people are that were there to help us put it up. We are no longer a curiosity.

The men from the village are pushing their pongas out into the water to start the day's fishing. They use old car axles with wheels on each end. Several men lift the bow of the boat and several others push the axle under it. Then

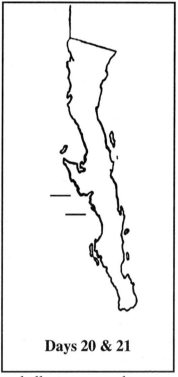

Days 20 & 21

they push the entire unit out into shallow water and remove the axle—very ingenious. The beach here is broad and flat, and we are camped a hundred yards from the water line of the now low tide.

As we carry our gear and boats to the edge of the water, we can see there are rocks spread throughout the surf line. The waves are only three feet high but it is a long surf line with three or four whitewater faces at any given time. That, combined with the reefs scattered here and there, will call for some good control as we paddle out.

At 7:20 a.m. we are through the surf and very clean, because we are submerged several times under the incoming waves as we thread our way through the rocks.

Behind the surf line the water is calm and filled with porpoise again. We don't follow the shore, but instead set a compass course across the bay for La Bocana. This will save us several miles of paddling. The afternoon wind comes up and we use the sails the last couple of hours to get us to Punto Arbriojas. We fold up the sails and paddle around the point. The wind is twenty knots from the north west and is coming directly over the point and into our faces again. This seems to be the normal circumstance every time we round a point.

The difference today is there are ten foot Pacific swells rolling in from the south about six seconds apart and pounding the beach. There are miles of shallow shoal water off Punta Arbriojas and the big swells are peaking and breaking across each shallow spot. The wind is blowing against the waves and tending to hold them up, so they are often rising twelve feet into the air before they crash down in a blue water curl you can almost see through.

These are bad breakers for us. This is stuff we can't handle if we get caught. As we paddle we study the water ahead of us and very carefully pick our way between areas of crashing foam. I pick up a thirty inch barracuda on my fishing line as we pass over one reef. I have to wait twenty minutes until we are out of harms way before I can pull it in. We tie it to the deck.

After another forty minutes of paddling we find an area about a quarter mile from town where, if we are careful, we can make it through the surf. We go for it and reach the beach in one piece.

On the paddle around the point we passed two large ships that were wrecked on the beach. It is easy to understand how they got here with all the shallow water and giant surf. We're happy not to be wrecked next to them.

We set up camp and get some water, refried beans, cookies, and tortillas in town. We put the tent up for protection from the blowing sand and use old tires we find on the beach to hold it down. One of the tires has a twelve inch rat in it. When I lift it up and start rolling the tire down the beach to get it back to camp, the rat stays in it, running on the inside as I roll it along. He looks like a hamster in a cage doing his exercises in one of those spinning wheels. When I lay the tire flat at camp the rat jumps out and runs down the beach. This is the first time any of us gets a good look at one of the critters that have been eating through all of our gear bags and even chewing on our fingers at night as we sleep. He is ugly and cute at the same time. A worthy advisary.

We huddle in the tent and cook our Top Ramen with today's barracuda in it for dinner. The blowing sand makes it impossible to use any electronic gear like the video or the camera. Our gear, which is piled around the outside of the tent, is being buried in the sand. I hope we can find all of it in the morning. Dave uses the boat as a wind break to sleep behind and the rest of us sleep in the tent. We hate this fine powdery sand. Microsand is, truly, the sand from hell.

DAY 21—JUNE 5, 1992

The morning is foggy and the sky is full of dust. Visibility is poor, perhaps two miles. We complete our normal routine and punch through the surf at 7:20 a.m. We seem to be within ten minutes of the same time every morning whether we hurry or not. We don't hurry this morning.

We set a compass course for Punta Holcombe at the mouth of San Ignacio Lagoon. By cutting straight across the bay we will save an hour of hard paddling. After a few hours we spot land. Everything seems fine. We put the sails up and cruise along without paddling for awhile. Our relaxed state changes, however, when Glenn says, "What's that out there to our right?"

We all look and there are breakers as far as we can see. There are breakers on the outside, in front of and behind us. The wind is blowing stronger now and we put away our sails to slow down our progress. We pull out our charts and try to figure out where we are. With the wind at our backs we are drifting rapidly along the coast, deeper into this pocket of waves, pondering our charts.

We come to the realization that we are just where we planned to be. The problem is we didn't take into consideration the waves breaking on the off-shore bar that projects eight miles out to sea. The swells are the same big ones we had to deal with coming around Punta Arbriojas. The shallow water caused by the onset of low tide is creating a line of ten foot breakers on the bar as far out as we can see. It is also starting to close in behind us. The lower the tide drops the bigger the breakers get. We either have to cross the bar or paddle back five miles to go around it by passing far out to sea. We decide we can pick our way through the wave line.

The wind is really blowing now on shore. Unlike yesterday, when the wind was holding the waves up so they would crash in a thunderous curl, the wind now is from behind the wave and is pushing the tops down the face early; and the white water is much softer as it slides down the wave. We think if we get caught in one of these we can survive and ride it out in a broach. The surf is only travelling about fifty yards and then flattening out again. We go for it.

We must paddle directly out to sea and into the wind so we will have as much room as possible to maneuver the boats when we start through the whitewater area. This is the first major bar crossing for any of us. I don't know how the others feel, but I'm more than just alert—I'm damned tense.

I think we will be through the breaker line in a few minutes but in reality the bar is much wider and more uneven than I realized from my low observation point in the boat. We all commit to the crossing and ride up the face of one giant wave after another. Some break just after we stick our bow through them and almost suck us back down the face. Others break a hundred yards from us and we outrun them, just making it past the roller as it goes by. This goes on for over an hour with both Glenn and I giving it everything we have, both physically and mentally. We shout back and forth, "Wave on the right"—"Outside"—"Steer right." Every once in awhile we see Jan and Dave climbing a wall of water and disappearing behind it as it turns to froth. At last we are through it.

We raft the boats together, eat lunch, and share stories of how each of us is more wonderful than the other. There is no way to express the feeling you get when you have just conquered something you're not sure you could. In this case, it was conquer or be in big trouble. We congratulate each other for remembering which "school of thought" we belong to, say, "Thank you, Tom Beal," and continue down the coast.

Our conversation turns to the similar experience we had a few days earlier when we weren't sure we were going to survive the landing on the "The Mother of all Beaches— The beach from hell." Jan says we need to give that beach a name. I recall a talk I went to at the Sea Kayak Symposium in Port Townsend, Washington, in 1991. It was by Joanne Turner, a lady who is responsible for running the largest kayak club around, with some one thousand members. She was talking about Baja. She made the comment, "Baja has so many lovely little coves to just pop into and have lunch." We decide to name our "beach from hell," "Playa de Joann." We certainly popped into it and we did eat there so we figure it fits all the criteria.

We are tired now and ready to go to shore. We look at the coast line and it is all sand beach as far as we can see so we just make a left turn and head in. The surf is moderate but no particular problem and soon we have camp set up. Again we use whale bones to hold the tent down.

The beach is very flat and we are at low tide now. We find one pismo clam on the beach as we carry the boats up. We make our camp a long way up the beach and hope it is far enough. The microsand again buries our gear, fills our ears, eyes, nose, and in general tries to make our lives miserable. But it fails.

We are in good spirits and enjoy our Top Ramen with the clam in it. We look forward to tomorrow so we can once again say, "Yesterday was a good day."

I sleep a little uneasy most of the night because the beach here is very flat and water has obviously washed over the entire area where we are camped during the high tides just four or five days ago. We calculate we should be one foot above high tide line before we go to bed but I find myself keeping one eye open most of the night. The wind is blowing off shore and that is good. The clouds look like a storm may be coming and that's bad.

Week Four

DAY 22—JUNE 6, 1992

I get up as do the others and we start our morning ceremony of 'carry and stuff.' This morning we have to dig our gear out. During the night the wind has buried everything beneath the loathsome microsand. We talk about the offshore wind as we load the boats. Could this be the big storm the fishermen told us they heard is coming? We'll find out in a little while. Now it is time to paddle. Glenn takes a six foot wave right in the face as we leave the beach. It breaks on our bow

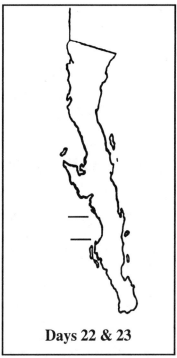

Days 22 & 23

and the entire boat and crew disappear for a few seconds. We pop out of the foam, with paddles flying in a blur, trying to make it past the next one before it breaks. We catch some air under our boat as we burst through the thin peak of the wave crest just before it crashes on its way to the beach. We check all of the gear we have strapped on deck and everything is still there. Jan and Dave have the sand washed out of their ears, too, as they punch through the surf line to join us. We decide to stay within a mile of shore as we paddle because of the offshore wind. If it is a big storm we don't want to be caught offshore where we can't make it back to the beach.

Two hours into our paddle some fishermen in a ponga see us and come over. They ask the same two questions.

"Where are you coming from? and "Where are you going?"

We tell them "San Diego," and "Cabo San Lucas."

One of them grabs his head and says, "Hijo Madre, en esta?"

We say, "Si, all the way in this," (pointing to our kayaks). They shake their heads, make motions to show strong arms, and hand us a big lobster.

They shout as they leave, "Muy peligroso, cuidado."

I know they are right. It could be a "very dangerous" trip, and we will be "careful."

After six hours the wind weakens and finally dies completely. This is not the big storm. We are happy. I can tell when we are all relaxed because we play Glenn's stupid word games. Jan and I aren't very good at them but we play just enough to confuse Glenn and Dave. Time passes and it is 4:30 p.m. Time for shore leave.

The beach is flat and there is a good surf running as far as we can see. It appears we can come in anywhere because it all looks the same from where we are. Dave spots a small sand mound that sticks up three feet higher than the rest of the beach. We decide to go for it because there are small bushes growing on it and we figure it is above high tide line. We turn hard left and paddle for shore.

We are expecting to have to maneuver through a long surf line because the beach appears a long way off, but instead the water becomes turbulent and confused. Waves break behind us as expected but then one breaks broadside to us. The water is bouncing up in sharp peaks all around us and we have to fight to stay upright. We don't understand what's going on but our only choice now is to keep paddling for shore. Suddenly we are on the sand, a hundred yards short of where we thought it was. We hop out of the boat and look around.

We have just crossed a sand bar in front of a lagoon mouth. We are standing just fifty yards from the entrance channel to the lagoon. We walk along the surf line and with lines pull the boats into the mouth of the lagoon. In the process one boat is knocked over by a wave in ankle deep water and we have to bail it out, but we have a beautiful campsite.

The surf is turbulent enough to dig up a six inch Pismo Clam. We pick it up and boil it in the pot with the lobster and Top Ramen for dinner. This is as close as we are going to get to bouillabaisse. Our camp is three feet above high water line and I will sleep better tonight.

DAY 23—JUNE 7, 1992

I wake up with a start as something is crawling up my arm. I don't move because I don't want to scare it. It doesn't feel like the mice that crawled on me before. It is bigger. I open my eyes slowly and strain to focus in the darkness on the creature which is now about to the elbow of my outstretched right arm. It is a crab. I had seen their holes in the sand when we were setting up camp. These are swimming crabs between three and four inches across. I am evidently sleeping in this one's territory. I lie very still, and he slowly continues up my arm.

When he gets to my shoulder, he is just two inches from my mouth. I gently blow on him. Like most animals in the wind he 'hunkers down' and holds on. I slowly take a deep breath and then blast him as hard as I can. He is lifted off my shoulder and falls on the ground. He jumps up, runs about two feet, stops and looks around. I can almost hear him thinking, "What the hell was that?" I move my arm and he scampers back to his hole, running sideways. I wonder if perhaps the Ninjas learned how to run sideways from the crabs. It doesn't matter much so I go back to sleep.

My crab doesn't come back and at dawn I get up and load my end of the boat again. The tide is lower this morning than it was when we came in yesterday and the waves are breaking in a serious manner on the bar. On the way out we catch air five times but get over most of the crests before they break. I can hear Jan and Dave's boat slap back into the water after catching some air right behind us.

We cover the fifteen miles to San Juanico in five hours and land on its beach to resupply. I stay with the boats. The others go looking for cookies. When they come back two hours later they have water, cookies, tortillas, and potatoes.

We meet some Americans in a van but don't ask them to call home because they are stoned out of their minds. We figure it would be a useless request. We climb back into our boats to take advantage of the afternoon wind to sail awhile.

In two hours we cover about seven miles and see what looks like a good place to come in. There is a large canyon that comes all the way to the beach. We go in right at its mouth. We encounter another small bar and cross it to find ourselves paddling right into a river mouth.

This is another great campsite. We see lots of crabs on the beach so we prepare mentally to be crawled on during the night. The only negative thing is the wind and the blowing microsand. Again our eyes, nose, and ears are filled with it, and we have come to just expect sand in all of our food. We have even talked about bringing back a bottle of microsand to sprinkle on our food for a few days when we get home so we won't have to quit cold turkey.

We sit around and tend our various miseries. The callus on Jan's foot that is tearing off must be very painful, but Jan doesn't complain and has kept it from being infected by putting Neosporin on it in the morning and at night. We keep the tube of Neosporin with our cooking gear so it is available every time we eat. We are all using it on some part of our body. Glenn has a rash on his butt that has to itch something awful, sitting on it in wet swim trunks all day. Dave's knee is all puffed up and stiff where he banged it on a rock, and my hands are swollen and sore from a combination of small infected nicks, sunburn, and arthritis.

It doesn't do any good to complain because we don't give each other any sympathy at all. If anyone complains about anything he is immediately deemed to be a wimp. Since our egos won't allow us to be wimps, we bear our various infirmities with a smile.

The crabs are active all night but we know they won't eat our clothes, make holes in our dry bags, or bite our fingers like the mice and rats do, so we just go to sleep and let them have the excitement of crawling all over us. Twice I wake up and shake my head to get a curious crab out of my hair. Now I know how Gulliver must have felt with all those little people walking on him.

DAY 24—JUNE 8, 1992

As we eat our oatmeal we talk about how close we are to Mag Bay. Reaching Bahia Magdalena will mean one hundred twenty-five miles of protected water for us to travel through. We are all looking forward to paddling on calm water instead of the five foot afternoon chop we have had for several weeks now. It is possible we can make it to the north entrance tonight if the weather stays good. Our concern then will be crossing the bar to get in. There is no passageway shown on the charts. We figure the Mexican fishermen must go in and out in their pongas and, if they can do it, so can we. All we have to do is locate the deep channel in the surf line.

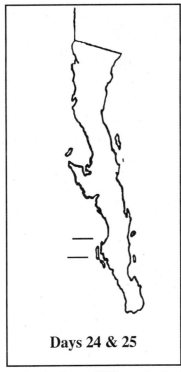

Days 24 & 25

We launch through a moderate surf and get all the dirt washed off us on the way out by a couple of cooperating waves. They are just big enough to give us a good bath without making us work too hard. We head down the coast.

The coast here is not interesting. It is rather featureless and it is hard for us to tell where we are on the charts.

After six hours of paddling, a fishing ponga comes alongside. We take the opportunity to ask the fishermen where the lighthouse is. I don't know the word for lighthouse so I ask them, "Where is the house of lights?"

They look confused for a few seconds and then their eyes light up as they realize what I want and how to help. They point south and say "ten kilometers."

They ask us, "Do you want us to tow you there?"

We thank them and say, "No, we are doing this for sport." They shake their heads and shout, "Adios" as their boat pulls away and races off to some fishing spot known only to them. We know where we are now. If the lighthouse is six miles in front of us, that means the Boca or mouth of the bay is fourteen miles in front of us. We decide to camp short of the entrance so we can negotiate the bar in the morning when it is calmer. If we get into trouble it will be safer at 10:00 a.m. than at 6:00 p.m. We would have more daylight time to solve any problems like gathering up gear from an overturned boat, swimming ashore, or just drying out our wet gear. We are anticipating a big bar like the one at San Ignacio.

We pass the lighthouse and go four miles farther before we camp. This puts us four miles from the place we hope to enter Mag Bay.

We land through moderate surf on a steep sand beach. The sand here is much coarser than on the other beaches we have been on recently and does not blow in the wind. We are so happy to be out of the microsand we don't mind the wind at all.

There are twenty foot high sand dunes behind the beach and we find a spot between several of them that is sheltered enough from the wind to build a campfire. This is only the second time in twenty-four days we have been able to have a fire. We lounge around and enjoy it very much.

Jan, Dave, and Glenn hike to the highest dune and call me over to see the north end of Mag Bay elongated into a channel extending behind our beach. We consider a portage but decide it would be close to half a mile through the swamp and it's not worth the effort. We will paddle across the bar and enter the bay tomorrow. We go back to our campfire and have our hot chocolate.

Each of us finds his own little hollow out of the wind and spreads out his sleeping bag. We put everything away in the boats before we turn in because the area is covered with coyote tracks. The coyotes aren't frightened of people down here in Baja. We have found their tracks just a few feet from our heads when we wake up in the morning on several occasions. Anything left out would be carried off by them. On a previous trip to Baja, Glenn had a camera carried a hundred yards out in the desert before the coyote dropped it. He only found it by accident. When we go to sleep tonight there is nothing left out to be carried away.

DAY 25—JUNE 9, 1992

When I wake up in the morning I see by the tracks in the sand we were right. The coyote came within three feet of me. He walked in a circle around me and then checked out the boat. Nothing is missing.

Our morning chores are finished quickly because we are anxious to leave here and get into Mag Bay. The water is smooth but there is a six foot Pacific swell running that is making respectable surf as it rolls onto our beach. Our entry through the surf takes concentration and we get thoroughly soaked but have no real problem. We are enjoying the surf washing over us now that the water is warm.

It is amazing how our attitude changes for the better as we keep moving farther south and the water gets warmer. Every morning the surf wakes us up, washes us off, and gets us going. We are becoming addicted to it.

An hour and fifteen minutes pass before we enter the whitewater of the bar. The entrance is called "Boca de las Animas." It is the most northerly entrance into Bahia Magdalena and is not used by yachts because the channel shifts and there is an extensive bar across the mouth. Sitting low in the kayak we can't see much except two to three foot whitewater breakers forming and dissipating. We raft the boats together and Glenn stands up to see better. He sees no channel. The waves and breakers seem to rise up and break randomly over the entire area. We assess the breakers and decide we can handle them. We head into the rapidly changing maze. It is only half a mile to reach the inside calm water of the bay.

Glenn and I enter the area from the north side and must work our way to the center before we turn into the entrance. If we turn too quickly or let ourselves get pushed sideways too far, we will get beached and not make the entrance. Dave and Jan take a course farther out to sea where they have more room to clear the shore. Glenn and I go directly in through the surf until we are in shallow water just off the beach, then turn hard right and angle back at a forty-five degree angle into the small in-shore break to work our way around the point into the channel. We lose sight of Dave and Jan about four hundred yards out but have no time to worry about them. It is all we can do to handle ourselves.

After ten minutes working along the in-shore break we enter the main channel and the wave size increases. As we pop up on top of a wave we see the other boat and then lose them as we broach down the wave face. The water over a bar is totally confused. Waves jump up from nowhere and in every direction. The wind is fifteen knots on shore. The tide is racing out of the channel against us and the wind. This slows our progress and extends the time we must spend in the slop. These conditions also peak the breakers up much steeper than normal. This definitely is not boring. Right in the middle of negotiating this mess my fishing line zaps out—I have a fish on. I have to ignore it for the present. I'm too busy surviving. Every time we get in turbulent water where we are busy trying to stay in control of our boat a fish hits our lure.

After twenty minutes we break into calm water and as I pull in my fish Glenn says, "I think there is something wrong with Dave's boat." I land the five pound pompano, tie it to the deck and look out to watch Dave and Jan's progress. They are doing fine but seem to be broaching all the waves instead of turning and running in between them when they have a chance. In a few minutes they reach us and Jan says with a disgusted look on his face, "The damn rudder broke again!"

Glenn said, "We thought you were just practicing your broaches." I add, "You were doing okay."

Dave replies, "Talent overcomes all obstacles."

Jan's reaction is, "Let's get to the beach and fix the damn thing—again."

We paddle a hundred yards in dead calm water to a sand beach. We get out, congratulate each other again on being wonderful kayakers, and eat a Snickers bar. Then we bend a new piece of bailing wire to fix the rudder steering cable.

With the calm water of the bay and the hundred and twenty-five miles of coarse sand beach that will stay on our right side only a hundred yards or so away, we are in fat city for a few days. No bad water to travel on, and a great camping spot anywhere we choose to stop. Suddenly another good thing is added to the list—we start catching fish on our drag lines.

Soon Dave has three nice corvina and I have two. We decide that's all we can eat and put the lines away. The mirror finished crocodile lure I gave Dave catches corvina almost every time. The feather I am using catches two small pompano for every corvina. Tomorrow I will change to a crocodile.

We paddle past Boca de Santo Domingo, which is the next entrance into the bay, and camp about three miles south of it. We look for firewood to build a fire, but this is a barrier island composed of all sand. There is no wood of any kind. We don't have a fire. We find a coyote's tracks on the beach and we wonder how it survives. There are lizards that bury themselves in the sand only to pop out when we walk near them to scamper at high speed over the next dune. These are undoubtedly a main source of food for our coyote friend. Their blood must also be the main source of the coyote's fluid intake. We decide we'll stick to water.

We have a dinner of Top Ramen and fish. I make the comment that, "It is just like the Sizzler—all you can eat."

Jan replies, "The salad bar here is really crappy."

Dave says, "Let's go to the dessert bar."

We break out the Snickers and eat an extra one, then it's hot chocolate time and we turn in for some needed rest.

DAY 26—JUNE 10, 1992

We are up and off the beach at 7:00 a.m. It's just a habit now. Even when we could sleep in we don't. The wind is blowing on shore with a vengeance. We stay within fifty feet of the barrier island shore to try to get some protection, but the island is composed of low sand dunes and affords very little relief from the stream of air whipping over it. I recall that protection from the wind is only five times the distance from an object as the object is high. If a mountain is one thousand feet high it will give protection up to five thousand

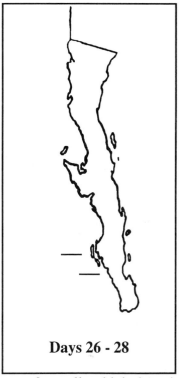

Days 26 - 28

feet from it. Our island is only ten feet tall, which doesn't help us very much. The water, however, is smooth if we stay close and that does help.

We have a good day fishing and have seven three pound Corvina when we land at 4:00 p.m. I change my lure and am not bothered by the little pompano like I was yesterday.

We set up camp and are able to find some driftwood. We roast our fish over an open fire. We passed Puerto Lopez Mateas today but didn't stop. It was across the bay and we didn't want to have to paddle back against the wind. We will be at San Carlos tomorrow and had no reason to stop today. I noticed as we paddled by Puerto Lopez Mateas the town was much bigger than it was in 1985 when my wife, Sharon, and I came here on a whale watching trip. It seemed to me to be at least double the size it was then.

We aren't pushing hard on our paddling while we are in the bay. Before we got here we talked about covering forty miles a day because we could do them quite easily in the calm water of the bay. Without having to worry about where to camp or capsizing coming to shore and having to dry our gear out we could just keep paddling to 7:00 p.m. Instead, we are averaging only twenty-five miles and getting caught up on our rest. We know we will still have a few hard days ahead of us when we leave the bay.

The highlight of our paddle today is a coyote. He is sitting on the shore as we paddle by. He just watches us. When we get within a hundred feet he gets up and wanders over the dune out of sight. Just about then Dave's rudder breaks again. We raft together and fix it. My rudder is bent slightly but still works, so I'm leaving it alone. I think it must have been bent by the surf coming across the bar.

We have a new pest in camp we haven't had before. A giant horsefly. It lands on me so gently I don't feel it. When I do feel it, it is too late because it has already taken a bite. I kill it with a quick swat but the blood is running down my leg anyway. The flies are all over us and all of us are bitten many times before we get smart and take refuge in our sleeping bags.

As I lie in my bag waiting for the sandman to come, I think of how adventure seems to be the very essence of my being. I have many times been told that I had been born one hundred years too late, but that's not true. I realize, as I lie here hiding from the flies, the problem is that I tolerated too much time between adventures. Even in our modern over populated world, there are hundreds of adventures waiting to be experienced. When I was younger it seemed I had enough time to get them all in so I didn't hurry. It doesn't seem that way any more and I realize I'm going to miss many of them I could have had. Too bad.

Our cooking gear was simple. One pot, one frying pan, one wind shield and a one burner MRS stove. Glenn is our chef.

DAY 27—JUNE 11, 1992

The wind is blowing from the west when I crawl out of my sanctuary, and the sand, even though it is not microsand, is blowing off the tops of the dunes and slowly burying us. This would be a bad place to build a house because the sand dune would slowly walk over it and it would disappear. We decide not to hang around long enough for that to happen, (about five years), and leave the beach at 7:00 a.m.

The wind is strong but directly off our starboard quarter so our sails are of no use to us. We paddle for four and one-half hours and turn to the east around the last point before San Carlos. Now the wind is at our backs. We extract the sails from the cockpits and increase our speed to five knots for the last forty-five minutes into town. About a mile from town Glenn and I notice Dave and Jan take down their sail and start paddling. We continue to sail on into shore. When they catch up with us we find their rudder had broken again. We select a beach in front of the cannery and next to the loading dock, because it is out of the wind, and land on it. We fix the rudder again with a new piece of bailing wire.

We seal up the boats and leave our wet shirts on top of them to dry out a little while we are gone. We enjoy the one mile walk into town. We ask about a phone and find there is only one public phone in town and it is closed from noon to 3:00 p.m. I look at my watch. It is 1:00 p.m. We buy milk, bakery stuff and tortillas and go to the town square. The only place to sit is on some cement blocks and on the curb, so we do, and eat our lunch. When it is almost time for the store to open where the phone is located, we get in line behind some crew members off a freighter from Croatia that is tied to the main pier. This is a regular phone like at home, not a radio phone like the one in Tortuga, and our connection is good. My wife isn't home but my mother-in-law is, and I give her all the news. We are all okay. We are ahead of schedule. We will arrive at Cabo San Lucas six days before we had planned to. Tell Sharon not to dilly-dally on the way down. I'll be waiting.

Glenn makes contact with his wife for the first time since we left home. We are in good spirits. We stop and buy some more bailing wire so we can keep Dave's rudder working. It breaks every day, but as long as we have enough wire we can keep fixing it.

When we arrive back at our boats we can tell things have been moved around. Someone has gone through our gear. The radios, cameras, binoculars and expensive stuff are all there. The only missing item is Jan's paddling shirt. It is a long-sleeved shirt he has been wearing to keep the sun and wind off of him. It isn't expensive and he can get along without it now that it is warm. It isn't really a big deal but it spoils the positive feeling we all had about this place.

We are all noticeably quieter and disappointed. Our trust has been violated and we just want to get out of here.

We push off the beach and head directly into the wind that was behind us when we sailed in. We only have to paddle two miles into it to get back to the lee side of the barrier island where we will make camp. The crew on the Croatian freighter are standing at the fantail of their ship as we paddle under them, waving at us and shaking their heads. It's a hard paddle, but we make the two miles in a little over an hour. We pull into a cove that has a few mangrove trees in it. It is a very attractive cove and a big mistake.

Dave and Glenn go diving and find two buckets full of little butter clams. We eat them for dinner along with our Top Ramen. We watch the sun go down and slide into our sleeping bags expecting a good night sleep.

I wake up about 11:00 p.m. I am covered with ants. They are inside my clothes and all over my body. I jump up, strip down, brush myself off, and shake out my bag and clothes. I move about thirty feet and try again. Because of the ants, I pull my bivy sack over my head. It has mosquito netting across the end of it and I pull the draw string to close the sack tight, and seal myself in. No more ants for me tonight. I am right. I sleep through until dawn and then I meet my next adversary.

DAY 28—JUNE 12, 1992

Slowly my mind wakes up, and before I can open my eyes I hear a buzzing. It is important at this point to inform the reader that I am quite hard of hearing. For me to hear a buzzing it has to be loud. I open my eyes and on the mosquito netting just inches from my eyeballs are a hundred mosquitos staring in at me and calling my name. I hate mosquitos. There is nothing I can do. I have to get up. I have a choice of wetting in my bag or being eaten by bugs. I choose the bugs. I figure my body will heal, but I have to keep my bag dry. I roll around the beach and shake as hard as I can to get the mosquitos off the bag. I must look like a gigantic Mexican jumping bean having a seizure on the beach. I pop out of the bag and run a hundred feet down the beach to escape the swarm around where I was sleeping. It is a good strategy. I only get three welts on my body before I get my clothes on and cover up all my skin. The others are moving fast and swatting as they pack.

I walk down to the water to wash my face and find coyote tracks coming from Dave's boat down to the water line. About a hundred feet from the boat I find Dave's dive mask, which had been left in the cockpit. It has teeth marks all over it and the strap is chewed clear through. A little farther down the beach is part of his wet suit, and a little farther one of our life vests. We gather up everything we can find and get all the gear back. Glenn has an extra mask strap and Dave is a diver again. We are going to have to put everything away each night even though we are sleeping right next to the gear. The coyote stole the diving equipment from within two feet of Dave's head while he slept. The mosquitos are still bad and we hurry to leave the beach.

The wind is blowing this morning like it has been the last three days but for us there is a big difference. The last two days we have been in narrow channels that weave and turn as they work their way south and the wind was coming from directly off our right side. We couldn't use the sails. The wind has stayed the same but the coastline has turned towards the east more and the wind is now at our backs. The bay has also opened up and we have more room to maneuver the boats. We paddle for the first mile to get us clear of shore before we put up the sails. We need to start out a ways in order to clear the point ahead of us.

This is the first day we have been able to start to sail in the morning. Normally if we use the sails at all it is only for an hour or so in the afternoon and then we usually have to paddle at the same time to make it worthwhile. Today the wind is not only in the right direction, but strong. It's blowing a good fifteen knots, perfect for sailing.

To our amazement it stays that way all day. We sail across the main entrance to Mag Bay and on to Isla Santa Margarita. About half the way along the shore of the island is a hook of land and the water channel narrows to four hundred yards. The wind is also compressed as it passes through this narrow spot and we pick up speed. We cover the water through the strait in a couple of minutes and turn hard right to tuck in behind the spit of land that formed it.

There is a small town here in the cove. On the finger of land projecting out into the water there is a large factory that appears to be a modern cannery but there is no one around anywhere. We think it is not fishing season and in a few months when fishing season opens this place will be a beehive of activity. We go ashore and have lunch on the beach, out of the wind, behind one of the big buildings. Lunch takes half an hour and we are soon under sail again, heading for the south end of the island. We go ashore on Punta Tosca, just inside the mouth of the bay. There is a large mangrove area here so we stop well short of it to camp. We may be slow learners but we're not dumb. We want to avoid the mosquitos.

The weather is sunny and warm even with the strong winds. We are wearing shorts and enjoying it. I feel something on my leg and look down. To my astonishment I see a five pound fly eating it. I swat the fly and kill it but the blood is running down my leg where he bit me. These are the same kind of flies we had a few nights ago. Jan swats and says, "Damn that was a big motha!" I put my long pants back on and my long-sleeved shirt. We all get four or five bites before the day is over. It is amazing that something as large as these horseflies can land on you and you can't feel them until they sink their proboscis into your body. We try to ignore them.

We sailed whenever the wind came from behind us and was strong enough to produce at least two whitecaps in different areas at the same time.

We climb the mountain behind the beach to get a look at the mouth of the bay. We will be paddling through it on our way out of the bay tomorrow. We can see a bar of considerable size and a large breaker area, but from our high vantage point we are able to locate a channel where the waves are smaller. We make a mental note of where it is in relationship to shore and go back to camp to have dinner.

Glenn is working on his stove. It seems to have died. It is an older MSR stove and has an aluminum center piece. One of the aluminum adjustments has frozen and can't be fixed. Glenn tells us how the stove was designed to be all brass but the manufacturer changed part of it to aluminum and screwed it up. Dave has his butane stove and we will use it and open fires to cook on for the rest of the trip. We have five nice fish we caught today on our troll lines so we build a fire and start roasting them for dinner.

This is not a comfortable campsite. The water comes up almost to the cliff and there is no flat spot on the side of the mountain. The ground is covered with stickers and rocks. I decide to sleep in the seaweed and trash that has washed up at the base of the cliff and hope the water doesn't come up that high during the night. Dave sleeps down on the beach with me. We tie our boats to some rocks so if the water comes up they won't drift off. Then we put our sleeping bags right next to them, as close as we can get to the cliff. Glenn and Jan find a spot somewhere on the hill.

We are all very careful as we put out our sleeping gear because the stickers will go right through the bags. I use a board to scrape my chosen spot as clean as I can. I crawl into the bag, relax, and stretch my arm out to the side— right onto a small piece of choya cactus. I decide, as I am pulling out the spines, to keep very still tonight and not roll around. I think this spot is the most unsatisfactory campsite so far on the trip. As I finally relax, I look up at the sky and watch several hundred Frigatebirds hovering in the updraft of the mountain. It is the last thing I remember as I drift off to sleep.

Week Five

DAY 29—JUNE 13, 1992

I don't sleep very well during the night. My left arm is giving me trouble. It keeps going numb and aching. My right hand hurts, too, where the cactus got it. I get up three times during the course of the night and walk around shaking and rubbing my arm and hand. I strained my shoulder yesterday while I was using the paddle as a rudder going through the strait. The boat was moving very fast and it took all my strength to hold the paddle as a rudder and control the boat. The strain must have been more severe than I

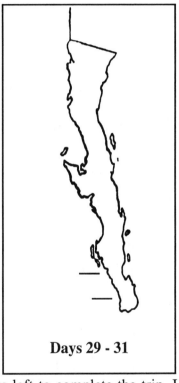

Days 29 - 31

realized. With only a few days left to complete the trip, I can't afford to have my body come apart now.

When I get up I notice that my right hand still hurts a lot from the cactus spines last night. I inspect it and pull out two more spines. I know I will feel better when I get in the boat and paddle for awhile. After an hour or so of paddling, I warm up the old carcass enough so most of my aches and pains go away. It's the same every day.

We leave the beach and work our way through the channel we spotted from the mountain the day before. We still have to pass through a surf line but it is only three feet instead of five feet.

We are now back in open ocean and enjoy the swell rolling under us again. After a couple of days we were all bored with paddling in the bay. The ocean is so much more alive and interesting.

We have a good day and make about thirty miles before we come in. We spot a river mouth and pick a spot just north of it. The breakers at the mouth of the river are eight feet high as they cross the bar. We avoid them and land a quarter of a mile south where the surf is only five feet.

There is a chunk of a sail boat half buried in the sand where we come ashore. It is the first twenty feet of the boat. Another twenty foot section is back in the estuary behind the river mouth, about a half mile away. We find the rudder section down the beach a little farther. It was a beautiful fifty foot boat at sometime in the past. Now it is just large pieces of driftwood washed up on the beach. A victim of what? Bad seamanship? A storm? Mechanical failure? We will never know.

The wind and microsand are a problem here but we take refuge between some large sand dunes. The wind is much less down in the hollow and we build a campfire. We cook our Top Ramen with dehydrated spaghetti sauce for dinner. This is a rather unusual combination. If you have never tried it, don't bother. We eat it up like it is prime rib. We are hungry. Our tortilla and peanut butter lunch was a long time ago.

Even with the wind and microsand this is a comfortable camp because of the protection given by the dunes. For lack of something else to do we check the condition of our hands and find they are all a mess. All of them are swollen and infected in one small place or another. Dave still has one good finger that isn't swollen or hurt. It is the only one amongst all of us.

My shoulder didn't give me any problems today as we paddled. I hope it lets me sleep tonight. We savor our hot chocolate and dig in for the night.

DAY 30—JUNE 14, 1992

I have a good night. My arm doesn't bother me as long as I lie on my right side and tuck it tightly against my body. Twice I wake up because the crabs are crawling on me, but I go right back to sleep.

I feel good when I get up and can tell the others are feeling good too. It's easy to tell when we are feeling good because we are a bit more insulting to each other than normal. Most people probably won't understand that statement, especially women, or for that matter, the new age male. The good old boys among you understand. You only insult people you love or hate. If you love them you make sure they know that before you insult them and your bond grows tighter. If you hate them you just insult them and hope they go away.

We are off the beach and paddling by 7:00 a.m. The sea is moderately sloppy. We play word games and discuss highly important topics for hours.

After seven and a half hours we have covered our twenty-five miles and solved all the world's problems so we look for a place of refuge for the night. We round a point, and as we hoped, the waves are a bit smaller in its protection. We come through the breakers with a lot of hollering and broaching and hop out on a poster perfect beach.

There is a round thatched palapa a hundred yards back on the beach. No one comes out of it as we carry the boats up the beach. We go to investigate.

It is deserted and has been for awhile. It is in good repair but the dirt is thick throughout from the blowing wind. It is forty feet in diameter with an eight foot diameter circular bar in the center. The roof is made from palm fronds peaked at the center on one giant pole. The floor is native rock set in cement and the outside wall is reeds standing on end and tied together to make a mat that surrounds the entire structure. The doors are just open spaces in the outer wall. There is no intra-structure. It is wide open inside. We move in for the night.

A Mexican drives up in an old pick-up. We ask him who owns our house. He tells us the Mexican Minister of Justice had it built for his family as a week-end beach house.

We are inside cooking pancakes when a young boy and girl come walking in. They speak no English and live on a farm somewhere back in the hills. We give them some pancakes and M & M's and they just sit and watch us for an hour. We find out the boy is sixteen years old and his sister, who is obviously pregnant, is fourteen years old.

They get up and leave but come right back with an old rusty twenty-two caliber single shot rifle and a very dead jackrabbit with a hole in its head. They bring these treasures in to share with us. We all make a big to do over the gun, the rabbit and especially the shot in the head. We find it interesting that they left the gun and the rabbit out in the desert when they first came in to see who we were. Were they afraid we were going to take them away? Was hunting or the gun illegal? We'll never know, but they did check us out before they showed anything to us.

Jan takes them out and shows them our boats and gear. He gives the boy a small hand compass he has carried as part of his survival gear. The boy is delighted.

The youngsters see we are low on water and say they have a well and will fill our containers for us. We start to go with them to carry the water back and they say no. They don't want us to come. They will bring it back. We wonder why they don't want us to come along.

I think I understand and tell the others of a conversation I had with a native deep in the jungle behind Mazatlan twenty years earlier. I wanted to take his picture and he said, "No." I asked him why he didn't want his picture taken. I was expecting some answer like "It will steal my soul," or "It is against my religion," or "It's okay if you pay me for it." I wasn't expecting the answer I got.

He said, "You will show it to your friends in the city and they will laugh at me."

I realized how insensitive I had been to their feelings. I had assumed because he was an uneducated native living in the jungle that he didn't have much in the way of feelings. I spent a week living in their village and found them to be the way we all should be—gentle, caring, and true to themselves and those around them. I have a beautiful portrait of him, with his permission, in my collection, and nobody laughs at it.

These young people were, I believe, ashamed of their meager possessions and humble way of living. They were embarrassed for the rich gringos to see where they lived. How wrong they were about us. If they only knew how much the four of us admired their simple lifestyle and them for being a part of it.

The boy came back just after dark with another boy he said was his neighbor, and brought us four gallons of water. We didn't see them again.

DAY 31—JUNE 15, 1992

When I wake up in the morning I always look for animal tracks to see how close something came to me while I slept. The mouse and crab tracks normally come up and over me, the rat tracks as a rule stay about a foot away and the coyotes rarely get closer than three feet.

This morning I see a new track only two feet from my face. Because of the dirt on the hard surface the tracks are very distinct and easy to recognize. It is a house cat. Jan has seen several feral house cats on his hikes in different areas. These wild cats have no problem surviving in the warm Baja climate. There are plenty of easy-to-catch mice and baby quail. The cat didn't bother our gear and we never saw it.

The surf off this beach is fairly crisp. We get slapped hard on the way out several times but the warm water feels good and we enjoy it.

There is no wind today and the coast is straight. There is no advantage to moving off shore to paddle. We stay a few hundred yards behind the surf and watch the beach as we travel. The beach is the same for thirty miles. We pass a lighthouse, which gives us a fix on where we are, but there are no other recognizable features. There are no pongas on the beach, and no human signs of any kind.

After eight hours it is time to stop, so we secure the gear on deck and start in.

The surf is big because this one hundred and fifty mile stretch of beach north of Cabo San Lucas is open to the Pacific swell and gets pounded constantly by waves from distant storms. Today the swells are eight to ten feet. They pose no problem at sea, but create big surf when they hit land. We figure we're ready for them and wait just behind the surf line, timing the waves like we do every day.

It's Glenn's call and when he says, "Now," we give it everything we've got and try to stay behind the wave in front of us and in front of the wave behind us. Sometimes it works. We are grunting as we strain to outrun the big mother that is on our tail, but to no avail. We are caught in a five foot whitewater face. Glenn reaches out in a brace stroke, the boat swings parallel to the face of the wave. I extend my paddle six feet out into the base of the wave just before it covers us. The only way to tell what is happening while you are under water is to feel the boat bouncing along and the pressure on your paddle as it slides on top of the still water under the wave.

Everything is feeling good and in twenty seconds or so we pop out in front of the wave. It is smaller now, as I put pressure on my paddle the bow swings around and the wave goes under us. We paddle hard but the next wave catches us. It is smaller, only about three feet. Just as we broach on it a third wave overtakes us and climbs up the back of our wave and buries us again. It is a bouncy ride but everything is okay. The wave is small now, only eighteen inches, and we are almost on the beach.

I am just about to swing the bow towards shore when we suddenly are upside down. I have no idea what happened. What I do know is my head is hitting the sand on the bottom. We are in less than two and a half feet of water. What I don't want to do is get crushed by the boat against the sand and hurt my shoulder or back. This is the kind of situation where it is easy to break an arm or a rib. I reach forward, yank my spray skirt off and bail out. I stand up in knee deep water.

Glenn is trying to get his paddle around to do a roll. It is a reflex action. He can't do it because the water is too shallow. He bails out, too. We pull the boat twenty feet to dry land, turn it over and dump the water out and wonder what the hell happened. Dave and Jan come in with no problem and we sit down and watch the beach to analyze what the problem was. Jan suggests that we just forgot what "school of thought" we belonged to, but we reject that theory.

As we watch the beach it becomes obvious what flipped us. The constant big surf has shaped the coarse sand beach in a steep face. When a large wave hits the beach it still has enough power to send water rushing up the sand. This same water loses its energy and changes direction to rush down the beach and back into the ocean. This creates a wave, in this case about two feet high, that is coming off the beach directly out to sea. As it hits the incoming wave they crash against each other throwing spray six feet high and dissipate.

We were paying attention to the small wave we were broached on when one of these reflective waves backsided us. Reflective waves are a characteristic of a steep beach. We should have been aware of that. We won't get caught like that again. The score now is one surf dump for each boat, but I have to admit that Dave and Jan outdid us with their end over ender.

This is a good campsite. The sand is coarse, there is no wind, and no trash or people anywhere. Behind the dunes there is a salt flat that stretches as far as we can see both north and south. That makes this beach inaccessible except by boat and the surf here is not ponga friendly. This beach is similar to Malarrimo as far as human traffic—very little.

We build a fire and cook our Top Ramen for dinner. We had a special lunch today of tortillas and a can of refried beans instead of peanut butter. Today was the last of the Snicker candy bars too. We have had a Snicker break as we paddle at 10:00 a.m. every day. We will miss it the next few days until we get to the cape.

It's been a good day and we are close now to completion of our project. When we are through with the trip I won't miss my sore hands or the eight hours a day of paddling, but I will miss the simplicity of life and my friends.

DAY 32—JUNE 16, 1992

The wind is from the south as I poke my nose out of my sleeping bag in the morning. The last few days the pattern seems to be south wind in the morning right in our faces as we paddle, but not strong enough to hurt us much. Around 10:30 a.m. it normally dies and the ocean gets dead calm.

We keep looking for a northwest wind to help us along but have no luck the last few days. We don't have the long land

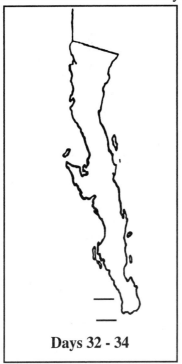

Days 32 - 34

mass in front of us any longer to heat up and create the on-shore flow that has helped us on several occasions in days past. Now our hope is that the southwind doesn't get so strong we can't paddle against it.

We are low on water and use all we have left to fill our deck bottles to drink as we travel today. The sun is hot now and we are drinking more water during the day than we have before. We will be able to find water in Todos Santos tonight. If we don't find any we'll have to make some with our desalination unit.

Packing the boats has been easier the last couple of days. The amount of food we are carrying is considerably less now and we are not replacing it because we are only a couple of days away from a big store in Cabo. Jan lets out a holler. "Look at this." He has found six more Snicker bars tucked away in his bow bag. We're all excited.

We're ready to leave the beach and turn our attention to the surf. The waves are big and crashing a long way out. Jan and Dave give Glenn and me a push and we go for it. These are big waves and when they hit us we have to dig in hard with the paddle to keep from being washed backwards.

As soon as we start I put the rudder down to give me control of the bow to make sure we hit each wave straight on. Three big waves try but none of them are successful at liquidating us. We heave to outside the breakers and turn to watch our two compadres.

They do not have the advantage of a push off the beach like we did and have to wait to be washed off. I remember how Glenn and I got pounded a few weeks earlier when we had a similar situation.

To make matters worse for them, Dave has decided not to use the rudder because of its weakened condition. He is afraid, and rightly so, that in its jury-rigged state it will break with the pressure of these big rollers on it. The swells pass under us and lift us up. We can see them on the beach. Finally a big wave reaches them and they are on their way. We see them punch through the first wave—then the second.

As we watch we are lifted by a giant swell that crests and crashes between the paddlers and us. It rolls to shore and they don't come through it. Then another giant one, and another. This is a major set. We don't see them anywhere. I say, "They have to be down."

Glenn says, "Hold the boat out here, don't let it get caught in one of these monsters. I'm going to swim in and help them get back to the beach."

Glenn loosens his spray skirt, looks up and shouts, "They're up!" I look and can see nothing but spray coming off the top of a breaker rolling to shore.

I say, "Are you sure?"

"Yes, I saw the tops of their paddles over that last wave. They're down the beach."

We paddle two hundred yards south, and finally the big set of waves passes and we're back to the normal five footers. The other boat comes into sight breaking through the back of a wave and dropping three feet into the next trough. They punch through the next one and make it over the last one before it can break. They are out of harm's way and join us.

"That was fantastic!" I shout.

"We thought you'd had it," shouts Glenn.

"So did we," answers Dave.

Jan says, "Never again. I don't ever want to go through that again. I hate to get wet."

It had taken them seven minutes of maximum effort. We counted six breakers of over seven feet to say nothing of the five footers, and they had been washed three hundred yards down the beach. Without their rudder they kept getting broached and washed backwards. They are slumped over in the cockpits, totally whipped.

I am reminded of an old painting of "The Last Indian" hanging on the wall of my aunt's house. It is a warrior slumped over his horse, totally worn out. These wave warriors are exhausted, but, unlike the Indian, they won the battle. We rest a few minutes so they can catch their breath, and once again we point the boats south.

We are thirty miles from Todos Santos but the water is calm and we plan to go all the way. Ten hours later we are looking at Punto Lobos ahead of us. Jan says, "We should be there in thirty minutes."

Glenn says, "John and I can make it in fifteen minutes."

"No way," is the answer. We've stopped paddling now and are all eyeballing the point.

Glenn makes the challenge. "I bet you my Snicker bar against yours that we can do it under fifteen minutes."

Jan says, "You're on."

I say to Glenn, "Do I get half the Snicker bar if we win?"

"A deal."

"Let's get this show on the road." We all synchronize our watches.

It is a long way and I'm not sure we can do it but we give it everything we've got. Even I am surprised at how fast we get the boat moving. As we close on the point we can see there are lots of pongas on the beach. There are also lots of people. The fishermen are getting in from their days work and there are twenty-five pongas and fifty or sixty people on the beach. They spot us when we are about a half mile out. Soon they are all watching us. The surf on the beach is a single shore break. It is not huge but it is devastating as it crashes on the sand.

As we approach the beach we don't slow down at all. The wave crashes two feet in front of us and we shoot up the sand right at their feet and hop out. I feel like Errol Flynn in some movie. The time is eleven and a half minutes. We won. I figure we used the energy in four Snickers bars to win one but it feels good to be a winner even if you are a dumb one.

Dave and Jan reach the beach and the Mexicans help them land. They get caught in the backwash and roll around in the surf a little bit. The fishermen think they are funny and laugh at them. It would be interesting to know what they really thought about these four crazy gringos that washed up on their beach. We set up camp between the pongas.

Dave, Jan, and Glenn have no trouble getting a ride into town, which is three miles away. They will have to walk back. I stay with the boats, pelicans, and wild dogs.

I sit on the beach all alone. Everyone has gone home. There are fifty or so pelicans twenty feet in front of me. There are wild dogs all over the beach. Like the pelicans they eat the trimmings from the fish that are left by the fishermen. They are frightened, scrawny animals of every breed known to man. Some are sick. Some are starving to death and some look healthy. The one thing they all have in common is they all look scroungy.

My mind recalls a story that Tom Brown tells in one of his survival books of a pack of wild dogs that chased him for most of a day. I also remember being chased by a pack of wild dogs on my bicycle once. I was on a racing bike and just barely got by them. I couldn't help but think of the five year old that was killed by wild dogs when I was in college right on the edge of Huntington Beach, California. I take a good look at the twenty or so dogs in the area. They are so beaten down and starved I don't think they would be a threat to a rabbit. I'm safe.

No one knows our inner most thoughts. Is Dave wondering how we are going to get through the surf, or why the ocean is salty?

The pelicans also have sick and dying ones in their midst. There are three dead pelicans on the beach near where I am sitting. One of them is partially eaten by the dogs. If there is reincarnation, I sure hope I don't come back as a Baja animal.

My kinsmen are back from town with water, a cake for me, and cookies. We celebrate by having refried beans with our Top Ramen tonight. We watch the silhouette of the pelicans against the sunset as we sip our hot chocolate.

We seal everything up in the boats so the dogs can't get it, and go to bed.

DAY 33—JUNE 17, 1992

I wake up to dogs barking and peek out of my bag. It is still dark but a faint light is in the east. Dawn is near. The dogs are barking at the cars that are arriving full of men. The fishermen's day starts early. We get up and move our gear down on the beach to get out of their way. As we eat our oatmeal we watch them launch their pongas.

These pongas are about twenty feet long, eight feet wide, and weigh about eight hundred pounds. The beach is steep, and there is a seven foot shore break that crashes right on the sand. We wonder how they are going to get their boats out through it. They don't seem concerned and load their gear into the boats, ready to go.

They have to carry gas about two hundred yards down the beach to reach the boats. Two men put an oar between them on their shoulders and carry a twelve gallon container hanging from it in the middle. The men work very hard carrying all their equipment to load the boats and then they get together and slide the boats down to the edge of the water.

When all twenty boats are loaded and sitting side by side at the edge of the water they take a hundred foot rope out of each boat and tie one end of the rope onto the back of their boat and the other end to the front of the next boat with the line coiled in between. We can't figure out what they are doing. When all the boats are tied together, all the men come down to the first boat and with much effort push it slowly out into the surf. They wait for a wave to crash on the beach right in front of them and as the water shoots up the steep beach they shove for all they're worth and hurl the boat through the next wave before it can break. The three men in the boat are rowing and paddling hard to get clear. They make it. I'm sure they never had any doubts about it.

On their stern is the rope tied to the bow of the next boat in line. The men in the first boat start their motor and the line becomes taught. The crew in the next boat gets ready, and as a wave breaks and rushes up the beach, they give a signal to the men in the boat on the other end of the rope. Their motor races and the boat on shore is dragged out through the surf.

They in turn use the same procedure to pull the next one and so on until all twenty boats are off the beach.

The process is simple, efficient, and shows great evolution of thought in the problem solving department. I wonder how many days they didn't go out because of bad surf or were pounded by the breakers, before someone came up with this procedure. The show is over, it is time for us to get off the beach too.

We do our PAP launch and I am catapulted off the beach by the other three. Jan is next, and then Dave and Glenn swim out and climb in the boats. The fishermen watch us from their boats and from shore. They are impressed with our method like we were impressed with theirs. They applaud. We wave goodbye to each other with mutual admiration and start our paddles moving south. Only two more days to go.

It's hard to tell we're moving all day long because the beach looks just the same. With a couple of exceptions, there are a hundred and twenty-five miles of uninhabited, uninterrupted sand beach. We paddle for eight and a half hours and the concensus is that's enough for today. We only have about six more hours to go tomorrow to finish.

We see an arroyo and head for the beach. The surf is big and is breaking very close to shore. The beach is steep and heavily undercut by the big breakers. The backwash off the beach is very heavy. Not a good place to land but, it's like this everywhere, so we have no choice. We remind each other to watch for reflected waves and head in.

Glenn and I linger for a few moments just behind the break and then put 'the pedal to the metal' just as a big wave crashes in front of us. We ride in behind it but can't quite out run the next one and it crashes on our stern, rolls up the boat and slams me in the back. My hat and glasses are ripped off but we maintain direction and fly up the beach. Glenn is getting out of his cockpit even before we touch the beach. I dig my paddle in the sand to keep us from being sucked back. Glenn is out and has the bow. I scramble out and we heave the boat up out of danger. We look over and see Dave and Jan shoot up the beach.

They aren't as fast as Glenn was and before they can exit, the boat is sucked back down the beach. We watch horrified as they slowly swing sideways and are carried back under a cresting eight foot giant. There is nothing any of us can do. Glenn says, "Oh no!"

I shout, "Get out of there!" which, of course is impossible, even if they could have heard me. The surf crashes directly on them and they disappear in the tube. We are running down the beach to get to them. In this shallow water, with the force of that wave and the heavy boat churning in the surf, they could be killed. The wave finally dissipates on the beach and we can see the bottom of their boat but no sign of them. Dave pops up. "Are you alright?" I shout.

"I think so," he answers.

"Where's Jan?" Seconds go by that seem like minutes. Jan appears out of the foam.

"Are you okay?" Glenn hollers at him.

"Yeah!" is all he can get out.

We all grab the boat, and whatever gear we can find floating. Jackets, shoes, water bottles, and hats are all rescued. I see a bag out in the surf. It keeps disappearing under the breakers. It takes me several tries but I finally find it between waves and bring it in. It is Dave's dive gear. Now we're even. Jan saved Glenn's dive gear the first night out, and I save Dave's the last night out.

We get all the gear we can find ashore and take an inventory. Jan lost his hat, and one of our water bags is gone but we won't need it now anyway. My hat came off but it was tied to my neck and my glasses were trapped inside the hat. The cord I had on the glasses was broken. I was lucky.

We inspect the boat. Both Jan and Dave say they heard a resounding cracking noise. On inspection they find the boat is literally broken in half. Right in front of the rear cockpit there is a complete break six inches long in the hull on both sides and the keel piece is broken clear through. We turn the boat upside down and the 'fix it' crew starts to work. Two hours later they have it all patched up with fiberglass and we are ready to go again. The seam isn't very strong but it is water tight and we only have one more surf entry and exit and we're there. If we can get off the beach tomorrow with no damage we'll be in good shape.

We find some cement bricks in a junk pile and build a fire pit. Dave caught a four foot needle fish today while we were in transit and we are going to roast him for dinner. He also caught a ten pound tuna that we released because we didn't need him to eat. These are the two biggest fish we have caught on the trip, and either one would have overfed all of us. I love to eat fish, but I only like it if it slept in the ocean the night before I eat it.

A van drives up on the beach. We realize there is a road that parallels the beach along here just a short distance away. There is a family in the van, a couple and their teenage boys. They are very nice gringos from Escondido, California.

They go surfing and we visit for awhile to get news of what's been going on back home. Mark, our new friend, makes me a margarita and the others drink pop. They decide to camp here on the beach near us. It is the first time we have shared a beach with someone else in thirty days. The last ones were Brian and Andromeda on Todos Santos Island.

We enjoy the company of Mark and his family just like we enjoyed our Todo Santos couple. Mark's wife, and I am embarrassed I can't remember her name, brings a salad over to us to eat with our fish. She says, "This is one thing you probably haven't been able to have on your trip." She is right. We love it, and really appreciate her kindness.

As we sit around our fire drinking our hot chocolate, I tell Jan he had me scared when the boat went over. He didn't come up for awhile. He says, "I've never been so scared in my life. Even when people were shooting at me during the war, I wasn't that piss-ass scared. I curled up in a ball and just held still until the boat got away from me." He had done the exact right thing. The heavy boat in that shallow water was a potential killer.

We have been very lucky on our entire trip. The weather has been about as good as it can get. When we have made mistakes, we have come through them without being hurt, and fortunately no one has become ill. After this capsize the score is Mother Nature three, kayakers zero, but we're still in the game.

It is a beautiful calm, clear, warm night. There is no wind to blow the sand and it is macrosand, not microsand. It doesn't get better than this. We turn in for the night and dream of Cabo San Lucas tomorrow.

DAY 34—JUNE 18, 1992

I wake up and it's still the middle of the night. I can tell by the position of the Big Dipper in the sky. Then I hear Glenn, a hundred feet away where he is bedded down, thrashing around and mumbling. I think he probably has some ants in his bag or something, and go back to sleep.

When I get up in the morning I ask, "What was all the commotion last night?"

Glenn says, "Pigs. Big pigs. I woke up and saw a huge pig rooting around our fire pit two feet from me. I picked up a stick and hit him. He jumped and ran about five feet, stopped, turned and looked right at me as if to say, 'What's with this stick shit? I've got some serious rooting to do around here and you had best turn over and go to sleep. If I get pissed, you'll be in deep trouble'."

What did you do?" I asked.

"What do you think?" I turned over and went back to sleep."

I told him he wasn't as dumb as he looks. He accused me of being a wimp or I would have come over to chase it away. Everything is normal, we are all in good spirits.

The surf is still very big and, because of our weakened boat, a real concern. We do a PAP launch. There is confusion as I get pushed off the beach because we all try to make the decision of when to go. The timing isn't quite right and I find myself facing a series of huge breakers. There is nothing I can do now, I'm committed. I give it everything I've got and just make it through three consecutive wave faces microseconds before they devour me. I fly the boat off the back of each of them. I hope Jan has better luck because his boat can't stand this intense pounding with its patched hull.

The timing is better on his launch and he makes it through with the boat in one piece. Dave and Glenn take a swim and join us. We start the final leg of our trip.

I notice several changes in our attitude as we paddle these last twenty miles. First, we are anxious. We keep thinking we are farther than we are. We think each point we pass is Cabo Falso.

The second change is we are all hurting. We complain about our hands, Glenn's elbow, Dave's knee, my foot, and Jan's uncomfortable seat. We have all had these and other discomforts the entire trip but now that it is almost over, it is okay to feel the pain. We don't have to suppress it anymore. I am sure if we had three more weeks to go we wouldn't hurt today. The mind protects us more than we realize.

As we cover the miles along the coast we see huge houses every now and then. These are gigantic estates hewn out of pure rock in some cases. "Big bucks," says Jan. We all agree.

We see many hammerhead sharks. This area at Cabo Falso is famous for them. They are all around us. We paddle over a couple of ten footers. We can see them clearly as they swim under the boat in the clear water. They are elegant specimens. Pure muscle and power. We see about thirty of them before we reach Arch Rock at Cabo San Lucas.

When we pull up alongside the glass bottom boat in the submarine garden off of the Arch Rock, we have made it. We have one more thing to do before we go ashore. We must say goodbye to the fifth member of our expedition, Judy.

Glenn takes the container with her ashes and hands it to me. "You get to do the honors, she was your cousin." I open the box, take out the plastic bag with the ashes and open it. Then I let the ashes sink into the beautiful marine garden that people from all over the world come to see. A fitting resting place for a pretty lady.

It is time now to paddle to shore and end this adventure. We paddle the three hundred yards around Arch Rock and come onto Lover's Beach. It is covered with people. Hundreds of people. We paddle in.

We get out of the boat and Glenn and Jan give a cheer. I join in from ten feet away and Dave tries to pretend he doesn't know us. The cheer goes, "One, two, three, four. Who the hell are we for? ME, ME, ME, ME." The people on the beach, being used to drunk gringos down here, just ignore us.

We carry the gear up the beach and take refuge in a small split between two rocks. Dave wants to go diving so the rest of us go into town to look around. Town is one mile away. We paddle the empty boats in. Dave stays with the gear.

We paddle into the harbor and find the entire harbor is a fancy marina. There is no visitor's dock so we carry the boats up a launch ramp, stash them on some broken concrete blocks, and walk into town. We see no Mexicans, just gringos on the street. We are hustled three times to buy real estate. We ask in a store where the bus station is and get a curt answer, "I don't have any idea." Not friendly at all.

We finally find the bus station in the old section of town and the people there are helpful. We need $150.00 to buy three bus tickets to Tijuana. We have $40.00 left. Glenn finds a place where, for a 10 percent premium, he gets $150.00 on his credit card. They buy their tickets. I call home and tell Sharon to hurry down, I'm already here. We paddle back to Lover's Beach and relax. The people on the beach think we are tourists and have rented a couple of kayaks from one the hotels. One asks me where we paddled from. I say, "San Diego." He replies, "oh sure!" and walks away.

By seven o'clock everyone is off the beach and gone back to their hotels and we are alone. This beach is isolated. The people get here by boat from the harbor, and they all have to get back before the last boat leaves.

We eat Top Ramen and talk about what we are going to do when we get home. I feel good about completing the trip. I feel bad it's over. I have a mixture of feelings I am sure are common on such occasions. We climb into our bags and sleep comes quickly. Tomorrow we have much to do.

DAY 35—JUNE 19, 1992

It never ceases to amaze me how easily we create habits and how hard they are to break. For absolutely no good reason we are all up at daylight. We eat our oatmeal and start packing. The difference now is we are packing to travel by bus, not by kayak.

In our last campsite at Lover's Beach, Cabo San Lucas, Jan sews up his pants so he can wear them home on the bus to Tijuana.

When Dave, Jan, and Glenn leave at 4:30 this afternoon everything that is left I will have to get into the harbor and load into my car when Sharon gets here in four days. They are carrying everything they can home with them to make my job easier. Every piece of equipment is wiped off and stored either in a bag to carry home or to leave here. We work until around noon and then all the bags that are going on the bus are loaded into my kayak. They help me launch through the tricky shore break and I paddle into the harbor.

The three of them hike over the mountain and meet me in the harbor.

We carry the gear a mile or so to the bus station and leave it there. We go back into town, get some fruit and bakery goods at the store and sit on the curb in the shade to eat lunch. We stroll across town and into one of the big hotels and sit in its lobby. We use its restroom to rinse our faces and our shirts in fresh water. It is the first time in thirty-four days.

It is a sad time. We have to say goodbye. The others want to take one last walk through town but I can't handle any more walking. My right foot is extremely sore and very painful to walk on. I don't know what is wrong with it and I'm just not up to suppressing any more pain.

We shake hands, say things I don't remember very well about what a good trip it was, and say goodbye. That moment is the only regret I have on the entire trip. We should have done something more, but we didn't. I limp off, with a tear in my eye, to my kayak to paddle back to Lover's Beach, and they wander off to kill time until the bus leaves.

I arrive back on the beach, now just one of several hundred. I repack the gear that is left, so it is equally distributed between the two boats. My problem now is going to be getting both boats back into the harbor when Sharon gets here. I have three days to figure out a solution and I still have $35.00 to last me until she arrives. I sit back in my chair, relax, and people watch.

The Finish

WAITING FOR SHARON

Now that my friends have left on the bus, I have three days, if everything goes well, to wait before Sharon can get here to pick me up. There is no way for her to contact me if there is a problem and that makes me a bit uneasy. I have told her I would meet her at the entrance to the harbor on the west side. There is an outdoor flea market there set up to sell over priced junk to the tourists off the cruise ships. Sharon and I had been there in 1985. My plan is to hang around the market until they arrived. This sounded simple as we discussed it in our living room before the trip started. Now, in real life, there are several irritating problems.

First, I don't know when Sharon is going to get here. She has another couple riding down in the car with her and I don't know if they will take turns driving and come straight down because they know I am waiting or if they will stop and see some of the sights as they had talked about before I left on the trip. If they drive most daylight hours they could make it by Saturday noon. If they look around the towns very much they could be as late as Monday evening.

The second irritation is the heat. It is hot and uncomfortable in town. There is no place to sit around the flea market except on a cement wall that is in the sun most of the day. My lower back is killing me. Because of my bad foot, it is painful to stand. I can't sit or stand comfortably and I don't know how long I am going to have to be here. One thing I don't do very well, even under the best of circumstances, is wait.

The third irritation is a potential problem. I don't have any money. I had $35.00 when the crew left. It will be enough if there is no delay being picked up, but if Sharon has any trouble and is delayed a few days I could run out of money completely. I have enough oatmeal and rice in the boat so I won't starve, but I am concerned. I decide to buy a small loaf of bread, a banana, and a quart of milk each day to live on. This will cost $1.50 and I can stretch my money out if need be.

The fourth item of concern has already become a problem. A storm surf is building from a hurricane south of us. I have to get the two boats off the beach and into the harbor. The surf is getting much bigger each day. I am worried about launching the boats by myself. They are both still heavy with gear and the surf in the cove is very tricky, with reflective waves rushing off a cliff face and traveling sideways across the incoming waves. The information I can get on the weather is that the storm is coming directly at us and will be here in a few days. I can't sit out a hurricane on Lover's Beach. I have to bring the boats into the harbor soon.

None of these concerns is of any major importance, but I am already feeling badly about the abrupt parting when the others left, and the heat is hard on me. My attitude is not the best. I try to stay in relatively good spirits but I have to really work at it. I spend the days looking for things that are funny, interesting, or attractive to look at. I only allow positive thoughts into my head. It is becoming a real struggle not to be depressed.

Friday morning I sit on the beach and take videos of the people coming and going from the boats. The action is funny because the boats, instead of landing, have the people jumping off into the surf. Often the people think they are in shallow water when they are not. Many submerge completely, purses, clothes, and all when they jump. Some get rolled severely in the surf and I am surprised no one gets badly hurt by a boat hitting them as they wash back and forth in the turbulance.

On Saturday afternoon I feel I have to go into town and wait because it is possible Sharon could arrive. I wait from noon to seven-thirty and then paddle back to the beach for the night. The surf is building more each day, making landing the boat touch-and-go when I come back. The boat is heavy and clumsy for one person to handle. I decide I have to get the boats off the beach in the morning. I will take them into the harbor.

At dawn I drag one boat down to the water and pull it out as far as I dare before I get in and seal up my cockpit. The first wave to reach me sucks me into a trough where I am spun around by another wave rolling sideways at me off the cliff face. I broach the wave from the side, take the shore break on the head and am washed back up the beach. I spin the boat around by digging a paddle into the sand, letting the water that is rushing back down the beach turn me. Then I go with it punching through the next shore break and am clear. I paddle for the harbor thinking one more boat to go and I've got it made.

I park the kayak in an empty slip and asked a worker on the dock about leaving it there. He says I will have to check in at the harbor master's office when it opens in two hours. He lets me through the gate to get off the dock and I start back for the other boat.

My plan is that to hike over the mountain back to the beach. The only problem is I don't know where the trail is. I look for it for half an hour and ask several people, none of whom has any idea. Finally one person says, "It's down by the water." After looking for awhile and not finding it, I decide to climb over the mountain without a trail. After all, it isn't a big mountain, how hard can it be? This is a bad decision.

I work my way up—up—up and finally get to the top only to find myself on a cliff face. I can see where I want to go. I will have to negotiate my way through the cactus and loose rocks on the face of the cliff to make it. Glenn, the mountain climber, would have loved it. I hate it. This is not my thing.

The sun is intense, already over one hundred degrees at 9 a.m., and I am sweating heavily. I have not planned on this kind of exertion and have not taken on any water before I started the climb. I am dehydrating rapidly. As I slowly work my way around the cliff, I do my best to avoid the cactus. My best isn't always good enough. I start to get dizzy from dehydration. I sit down and rest until my equilibrium comes back. I have to do this twice before I come to a place where I can see the trail I am supposed to be on. It is in a ravine right below and in front of me.

I am so happy to see it I shout out "all right!" and lean on a rock to rest a moment before climbing down to it. The rock comes loose and I tumble ten feet through the cactus to the edge of a fifty foot drop-off. I slide to a stop just two feet from the edge. What comes over me is a strange sensation. I know I have to crawl back up the cliff but I am frozen, frightened to move. I'm afraid I will start to slide again and it will be all over. I can see the headlines in the newspaper: "Kayaker dies falling off a cliff." I decide that will be too confusing for the general public to understand and I had better get out of here.

I don't know how to describe the climbing technique I use but it might be called a finger walk. My arms are stretched out in front of me and I move nothing but my fingers to pull me away from the edge. I try to think of other things so I won't freeze up again. I picture what I must look like inching my way up the cliff. What comes to mind are some of the scenes from the roadrunner cartoons where the coyote is bug-eyed and trying to escape some predicament. I have to laugh. It clears my head and I am okay. I make it back to the beach.

Launching the second boat goes better than the first one and I make it through the surf with no undue excitement. I paddle into the harbor and, for the first time, take a really good look at it. There is no place to land the boat on the dock and go ashore except through a locked gate and I don't have a key.

I go ashore at the boat launch ramp and walk up to the harbor master's office. It is early Sunday morning. As I walk up I see the lady turn the closed sign over to read open. I am hot, dehydrated, and very tired. My face is flushed and cactus spines are sticking out of my clothes. I'm sure I look a mess.

The lady behind the desk is by herself and is a gringo. She greets me with a big smile, and an upbeat "Good morning! What can I do for you?" It is amazing how much her cheeriness rubs off on me. I instantly feel a lot better. I tell her I have two kayaks in the harbor and I need to tie them up for the night. She says their minimum fee is $27.00 a night per boat. My cheeriness is gone again. I only have $31.00 in my pocket.

I know I have to stay in the harbor. I have looked around as I paddled in, and there is no place for me to hide the boats in the harbor, so I will have to pay somehow. I don't think I can manage the surf back on the beach; I am just too tired.

I think for a minute and then tell her, with a smile, "I have made a mistake. I don't really have two kayaks. What I really have is one catamaran. It is twenty feet long and six feet wide."

She says, also with a smile, "Well then, that will be just $27.00." I pay her the money and that leaves me with $4.00 in my pocket. I have to be out of the slip by noon the next day or pay again. I sure am hoping Sharon will make it by then. If not, I am going to have to drift around the harbor in my catamaran until she gets here.

I sit in the flea market all day and come back to the dock when it gets dark. The only place I can find to sleep is on the cement dock next to the boats. I get my sleeping bag out and go to bed. Sometime during the night I am awakened by two men talking. They walk up to where I am lying on the dock. I don't realize it but they haven't seen me. I sit up rather abruptly and scare them to death. They both let out a holler and jump three feet in the air. We all have a good laugh and I tell them the kayaks are mine. They leave and I go back to sleep.

In the morning when I wake up I go directly out to the main highway coming into town. Sharon will have to come into town on that road and I can head her off there and save having to walk a mile to the flea market. The boats are at this end of town now, not down at the harbor entrance and it will be much more convenient if I can catch Sharon as she enters town.

As time passes I get more nervous. If she isn't here by noon I will have to start floating around in the boats. I don't want to have to do that.

At 11:00 a.m. we spot each other at the same time. I hop into the car and feel instantly better than I have for several days. She turns the car around and pulls down to the launch ramp and parks. I say hello to Ted and Marge and give Sharon a big kiss. I go check out with the harbor master and bring the boats around to the ramp. We unload them and stuff all the gear into the Bronco. The boats get tied on top of the camper and we start the drive back to La Paz.

On the trip back Sharon tells me about the drive down. She had two exciting happenings. The road is very narrow and a truck passing them going the same direction, ripped off the side view mirror of our car. Like true adventurers they taped a make-up mirror to the broken mirror support and continued down the highway. The road is in poor repair from time to time. On another occasion she got a front wheel caught in a deep rut and ran off the road into the desert. They were lucky and didn't tip over or break an axle. A pick-up truck did the same thing a short distance past them and the rear end of the truck was ripped out.

The trip home is uneventful except for a delightful stop we make with some friends that are camped north of Loreto. Some of my ex-students from over the years gather together and go down to Baja every year for a week to camp and fish. They treat us like royalty and wine and dine us in fine style. It makes me feel good to know I was the one that first introduced them to Baja through my field classes in the summer. They have enjoyed it through the years as much as I have.

When we arrive back in California, we distribute the gear to its owners. I don't get a chance to see Jan or Glenn. I do see Dave but only for a few minutes. We leave immediately for Washington and home. We have a summer full of guests arriving and the first ones are due in just over a week. We have to get the yard repaired after neglecting it for two months.

When I find myself mowing the lawn I know for sure my Baja adventure is over.

Epilogue

Now that the trip is over and I am back comfortably settled in my Washington home, cutting the grass, planting my garden, and taking golf lessons, the adventure seems a long time ago. What did I learn and was it worth the effort? Would I do it again? What was my favorite place? What was my least favorite place? What's next? These are questions I have been asked by others as well as by myself. This is how I feel about them now.

WHAT DID I LEARN AND WAS IT WORTH THE EFFORT?

Life is the best school of all and an adventure that takes you to your limit in some area is the best classroom. In that context this was a good trip. I discovered I was more physically able than I had thought I was. This was a physically demanding trip and I had no problem with it at all. I found that I wasn't even close to my limits. It was the same for all of us. None of us came even close to physical exhaustion. All of the small discomforts we just worked through. We stayed within a relatively high comfort level for the type of trip we were on. We averaged twenty-nine and four-tenths miles a day for thirty-three and a half days. We could have stretched it to forty miles a day and still been in good shape. Our comfort level would have taken a nose dive, but would still have been within tolerable limits.

Others will eventually do it faster than we did just so they can say they hold the time record. That's the way it should be. The four of us will smile to ourselves and know we are responsible for their suffering a lot of pain and discomfort and that's the way it should be, too.

I learned that I am far more capable than I thought I was. I know now I can paddle anywhere in the world I want to. Distance is not a factor, only time is. Comfort is not a factor, only time is. My mother used to tell me, "Johnnie, you can do anything in this world you want to. All it takes is believing in yourself and being able to make a commitment." It is too bad there is not enough time in some of our lives to learn that. Whatever success I have had in life I have had because I believed her.

So what did I learn from this trip? I learned my mother was right and anytime you can prove your mother right, it's worth the effort. Let's see what other benefits were gained.

I understand to a greater extent some of the feats of the explorers and adventurers of the past I have read about. The books often call their accomplishments "super human." I believe their performance was not super human. I believe they were just humans living closer to their potential than the rest of us.

I learned, even at my age, I still have the ability to adapt to my environment and enjoy nature for what it is, not for how I had changed it. After being confined in a city for most of my life, I wasn't sure I could still handle nature without wanting to change it. There is no unchanged nature in the city. At home we complain the bed is too hard or too soft. The food is overcooked or not cooked enough. Our clothes are too wrinkled or don't match. If we ever stop to think about why we complain about these things we'd see it's because we have nothing else to do. None of these are important.

According to Maslow's "Hierarchy of Needs," when there are truly important things to consider, like will we be able to eat tomorrow or will we be alive tomorrow, we don't complain about the non-important things. A trip like this one helped to bring into focus the things that are important in life. I am more tolerant of trivia around me than I was before our paddle. I am less tolerant of people that complain all the time.

WOULD I DO IT AGAIN?

This is a tough question. No, I wouldn't do it again in the same way. There would be no reason to—I've already done it. That doesn't mean, however, that I wouldn't do it again. It would be a good three month trip—a trip where you stay on all the good beaches for a few days and get to know the fishermen a little. But I think there are too many other places I have not been to take the time to do that. I will probably paddle parts of it again just in a vacation mode, but I don't expect I will ever do the entire distance again. There are parts of the trip I want to show to Sharon, so we may take a few short trips together to some of the better areas.

WHAT WAS MY FAVORITE PLACE?

There were several good places. What makes a "good place" in my mind? It has to be fairly, if not completely, isolated. It must have a good beach to camp on. It must have some protection from the wind. It must have easy access to good fishing and diving. It must have a protected beach with minimal surf.

The only place that fits all these criteria would be Playa Santa Maria. The south end of Isla Geronimo didn't have a good place to camp, but would meet all of the others.

There were also several good looking coves twenty to forty miles north of Santa Rosalillita but we didn't go ashore in any of them. That would be a good area to paddle in for a week or two and just meander from cove to cove.

Playa Santa Maria, at least the small part of it we were on, was isolated by lava flows and we saw no dirt roads anywhere near the area. Our beach was seventy-five feet across the front and totally protected from all except south winds. Clean white sand stretched back about one hundred fifty feet to the lava flow that gave protection from the north wind with its ten foot high wall. The point on the west side extended three hundred yards to the south and the water behind it is dead calm even though the water on the other side, only two hundred yards away, was pounding on the shore and whitecapping heavily. The water was clear and there were many fish and lobsters inside the point in calm water. I got the impression from the others, as we talked about the trip on the beach at Cabo, that this was their favorite spot also. I think I'll go back there.

WHAT WAS MY LEAST FAVORITE PLACE?

By taking the same criteria for the best place we can find the worst place. There were several places that seem to be tied for this position. There were a set of conditions we contended with about six or seven nights that made life more difficult for us, a flat, unprotected, microsand beach in a high wind.

The areas where we had these conditions most of the time were around San Ignacio Lagoon and just south of Magdalena Bay. The wind created rough surf for us to penetrate on both landings and launches. The sand was constantly blowing through the air like rain in a bad storm. All of our food was laced with sand. Our sleeping bags were full of sand. Our ears, eyes, and nose were full of sand, and any equipment left lying on the beach was covered with sand and disappeared in less than an hour. We would stack all of our equipment on a tarp so when we packed up in the morning we could dig out the equipment down to the tarp and know we had it all. I could not take pictures under these conditions, so much of the trip is not documented on film.

All of the shorelines south of Magdalena Bay was steep sand beach. This means there was a single big crashing wave right at the beach. It is tricky to get through and in fact Dave's boat broke in half when they got caught under one. Getting out through these conditions is tricky too. It was also these conditions that forced us to come up with the PAP's launch. Fortunately, we never had to put up with a PAP smear.

All in all I can't pick out one place that was the worst. I was the most frightened when I was shot up on the rocks at Playa de Joanne, but I was the most uncomfortable dealing with the wind and the microsand.

WHAT'S NEXT

My next adventure I believe will be to explore Belize Inlet in British Columbia. It is on the mainland north of Vancouver Island. It hasn't been charted and looks very isolated on the maps. The loggers work back there, but not very many others ever get past Thunder Rock, which is at the entrance. Both Seymore Inlet and Belize Inlet on the other side of Thunder Rock interest me. It would take about two months to do it right and produce a good kayaker's guide to the area.

I am also considering a ride across the United States with Sharon on our tandem bicycle. I'm not sure, however, if she is considering it.

The Participants

Jan Richardson

The Human Animal's spirit lives to return from whence it came, nature. It doesn't matter to what extent man returns as long as one allows for the experience...at least once in his life.

After months of talking, preparation and finally packing on the day of departure, paddling past the San Diego breakwater, I asked myself the infamous question, "What the hell am I doing here!" The answer came little over a month later. Thirty-three days after we put to sea and after paying a token price, mentally and physically, I had the answer. I'd become involved with man's primal home with a minimum of equipment; seen the yet unspoiled wonders, lagoons with their own ecosystems, pristine; arroyos with ten or more varieties of cacti, one with wild mare and colt romping free; seen the desecration my fellow human animals perpetrated. (Those damn drift nets and cut and fill development) I had allowed my inner spirit to sour, to go back in ages, to become at peace with the environment from which we derive, the ocean who's waters our blood mimics.

The stark beauty of the Baja coast, high walled cliffs, steep rock beaches and sand-dunes made of sand so fine, when driven by wind polished teeth, was only matched by the friendliness of the Pescadoras. The Mexican fisherman—while not understanding the *Why*, the reason for the our trip—did know full well the dangers of the elements the loco gringos faced. In the same breath, let me thank John for the opportunity to return to nature and the pleasure of being tutored, by a great teacher of natural science, in the fragility of mother earth. To my other mates, Dave and Glenn, thanks for putting up with my weirdness in those endless hours of "what am I thing." I still have one Snicker bar to start the next excursion!

A humble THANK YOU goes to mother nature and her daughter, the Pacific, for obliging the four paddlers with fair weather. A 1000 miles, a 1000 smiles.

Glenn Pinson

In the Winter of 1987, Darren Jeffries and I embarked on a trip by kayak from San Felipe, Mexico with the intention of going down Baja. By the time we reached Mulege, we had also reached a philosophical breaking point and had to compromise on how we would finish our trip at Cabo San Lucas. We slowed down so we could enjoy the people and sights and in seven weeks we were in Cabo under the southern sun.

In the time following my return, the thought of going back down and finishing my journey around Baja nagged at me so I contacted John and proposed that he and I kayak the Pacific Coast. He seemed the natural choice for a partner since it was he who first introduced me to Baja and since he had the most survival and sea experience of anyone I knew. John attacked kayaking with a vengeance, taking lessons, buying a personal fleet of boats and generally learning everything he could absorb about kayaking. We paddled once together before our trip and that was the extent of my kayaking between 1988 and 1992.

Although I felt strong and ready to go, I soon learned that my paddling style differed a great deal from John's and so for the rest of our trip I learned what tandem boats are all about. They are about teamwork and they are about compromise, as was our trip. As John had the rear position in our boat and the most sea experience, he became the undeclared captain of our craft and leader of our trip. Most decisions were made ultimately by John and I think that most of the time we were comfortable with this. I know that we were not all in agreement all of the time, but even with its faults, a quasi-dictatorship works better than anarchy.

In planning our trip John had made marks every twenty-five nautical miles on our charts just to give us an idea what our progress might be. It became clear within a week that we would try to make twenty-five miles per day if at all possible. Though extra days for layovers were figured into our overall time frame, we had good paddling weather and seemed to become servants to our charts. After having dealt with this very issue on my previous journey, I felt trapped, and was unhappy with the situation. I soon became reacquainted with the routine nature of paddling, and became bored.

My negative feelings passed gradually away in a couple of weeks as I dealt with the reality of partners who shared different expectations. Teamwork was the oil that kept the machine running. I believe that there was never a time where a lack of teamwork became a problem. I only hope that any negative feelings I had did not affect the others. I do swear to myself that never again will I rush through a trip. I also know that as the weeks passed away there was much talk of relaxed trips to small islands with no thought of twenty-five miles to make.

Though we all stayed on the same beaches and moved on the same ocean, we each had different favorite times and places during our journey. My favorites always involved our whole team and I feel that we had a true melting pot of types that always kept us on our toes. I have not played a good game of "twenty questions" since our trip. I tell you I am thinking of something, it just might be a motley crew that was bound to reach Cabo come hell or high water.

Dave Seymour

Because of the economy slow down in 1991 I was finding myself more semi-employed than employed. When Jan told me that John had asked me to go on the Baja paddle it sounded like a good way to get out of the "ho hum" rut I was in. It was something to do that was not work oriented.

Living a basic, hand to mouth life style, was very appealing to me. The worst part of the entire trip was the last few days when I knew the end was eminent, and I would have to get back to my other life as a normal person. In reality I never got back to my "other life." I found my priorities had changed. Things like trying to have the ultimate car now seemed silly and immature to me. I am now a full time kayak person, leading tours, giving lessons, and working in a shop.

I had two favorite places on the trip. The first was the south end of Isla Geronimo, because of its mini fjords we dove in. They were beautiful and full of fish and lobster. The second was the "Beach from Hell." Landing on the beach was the high point of the trip for me. You might say, it was the adventure I was looking for on the trip. It took all our training and experience to make it. It is one of those thirty-second periods in your life that stays vivid forever in your memory.

This was also my least favorite beach. Sleeping on sharp boulders, on a hillside, with rats biting my fingers when I was lucky enough to get to sleep, was not my idea of a good campsite.

The best of the trip was getting to know three other individuals totally and completely. It takes this kind of experience to break through all the protective shields we cover ourselves with. The four of us were totally bare to each other. True friendship is most difficult to find, and I feel the four of us had obtained that level.

Was the trip worth while? In every way for me.

To order additional copies of these fine books
by John Reseck, Jr.
please complete the order form below

(Please Print)   Date _____

Name _____

Address _____

City _____ State _____ Zip _____

Phone (_____) _____

	PRICE	QTY.	AMOUNT

SCUBA, Safe and Simple
John Reseck, Jr.
  This diver's classic has sold over 50,000 copies
  since its first edition in 1975. It is packed full of
  skills not covered in SCUBA classes. Revised in
  1990 this book has become a classic because
  of its insight and accuracy, fun, informative, and
  enjoyable reading. Thousands of copies have
  sold at $12.95, now reduced to $8.00 - Don't
  miss this bargain!
	$ 8.00		

We Survived Yesterday
John Reseck, Jr.
  Detached from civilization, paddling nine hours a
  day, this 1200-mile voyage from San Diego to
  Cabo San Lucas, Mexico becomes an adventure
  of epic proportions both in survival and humility.
  Join the author each day as he challenges and
  overcomes challenges along the way.
	$12.95		

	Sub-total		
	Washington residents add 7.8% sales tax		
	Shipping		2.00
	TOTAL		

Send order along with
check or money order for
total amount to:

**Reseck Enterprises
631 Montgomery Lane
Port Ludlow, WA 98365**